NELSON THORNES
DRAMASCRIPTS

THE SPACEMAN

Rob John

Nelson Thornes

Published in 2013 by:
Nelson Thornes Ltd
Delta Place
27 Bath Road
CHELTENHAM
GL53 7TH
United Kingdom

13 14 15 16 17 / 10 9 8 7 6 5 4 3 2 1

A catalogue record for this book is available from the British Library

ISBN 978 1 4085 1977 6

Page make-up by OKS Prepress, India

Printed in China

CONTENTS

Introduction   iv

Acknowledgements   vi

The Characters   vii

The Spaceman   1

Activities   76

   Things to talk about   76

   Things to write about   77

   Bringing the play to life   78

   Staging the play   82

   Exploring the issues   84

   The Space Race   86

INTRODUCTION

Dramascripts is a series of plays for use in the English classroom and the drama studio. The plays have been written by playwrights who share a delight in live performance and the challenges it offers to actors, designers, directors and, of course, audiences.

Most of the plays in the series were written for professional companies. All are included because they tell stories and use techniques which will interest, excite and offer new insights to young people who are just coming to understand how drama works as an art form.

The range of plays in the series addresses the requirement to give students at Key Stages 3 and 4 an opportunity to study a variety of dramatic genres. The fact that they were all written for performance (and have indeed all been performed) means that they will also offer students the chance to understand how and why playscripts are different from novels. The activities presented after the script are designed to draw attention to this and to extend students' abilities in reading, writing and, of course, performing drama.

Many of the tasks invite students to use practical work to engage directly with the text or to formulate their own creative responses to its form and content. Others focus on the importance of discussing, writing and designing. Both English and drama specialists will find the series a valuable resource for promoting dramatic literacy – and simply performing the plays wouldn't be a bad thing either!

THE SPACEMAN

In the 1960s, nearly every eleven-year-old in England took an exam. The Eleven Plus was designed to 'select' children for different kinds of school, for different kinds of education and different kinds of opportunity. About 20 per cent of children passed and went to grammar schools, those who failed this test went to secondary modern schools. Parents of eleven-year-olds knew that a letter, which would fall onto the doormat sometime in April, could change their child's life for ever.

In April 1961, like Maggie, Michael and the others, I got my Eleven Plus letter. A few days later, I first heard the name Yuri Gagarin. The two events have been linked in my memory ever since.

I always wanted to write a play about the Eleven Plus. Even as a child, it made me angry. It seemed to me to be a cruel and stupid thing to do to children. When I went to school on the morning of the results, some of us still hadn't had our letters. I remember one boy's mother coming into the classroom to collect her son so she could give him the bad news at home. You could see she'd been crying. I passed and went to grammar school. All my friends failed, even though I knew that some of them were much cleverer than me. I very soon lost contact with them all.

Yuri Gagarin remained an obsession for me. We knew that the Americans had selected a group of test pilots and were training them to go into space. My friends and I had photographs of them. We knew their names and used to take bets on which one would get into space first. Then, from out of nowhere, came a Russian: Yuri Gagarin. I immediately became a fan. It wasn't because he was Russian. I just loved Yuri because he was the first.

I never knew that three months after going into space he actually came to London. I didn't find out until I was much older. It's still an amazing thought to me that when I was eleven, Yuri came within thirty miles of my house. I wish I'd seen him. I 'should have been there'.

Rob John,
August 2012

ACKNOWLEDGEMENTS

The author and the publisher would like to thank the following for permission to reproduce material:

p.78 Neil Armstrong clerihew by John Foster from *The Works* (ed. Paul Cookson), Macmillan, 2000.

p.85 Roger McGough, 'Streemin', from *In the Glassroom*, Jonathan Cape, 1976.

p.86 The Art Archive/Alamy, photo of Wright Bros plane.

p.87 Military Images/Alamy, photo of World War Two bomber.

p.88 RIA Novosti/Alamy, photo of Yuri Gagarin.

p.89 Bettmann/Corbis, photo of Neil Armstrong.

p.91 Derek Stuart, 'The Space Race', from Spaceways (ed. John Foster), Oxford University Press, 1986.

p.91 John Kitching, 'The Swirling World', from Spaceways (ed. John Foster), Oxford University Press, 1986.

Every effort has been made to trace the copyright holders but if any have been inadvertently overlooked the publisher will be pleased to make the necessary arrangements at the first opportunity.

THE CHARACTERS

MAGGIE

MICHAEL

STEVEN

JEN

VAL

CHRISTINE

JACKIE

JANET

TREV

CHRISTOPHER

DAVID

CLASS AND YURI FAN CLUB

VOICES

HEAD TEACHER

MISS GREEN

CHRISTINE'S FATHER

CHRISTINE'S MOTHER

JACKIE'S MUM

FIRST PRODUCTION

The Spaceman was first performed in March 1998 by Far East Theatre Company at Paston Sixth Form College in Norfolk. The same cast toured the production to schools and theatres in the East of England region later that year.

Jane Cunningham	**MAGGIE**
Andy Young	**MICHAEL**
Tim Bell	**STEVEN**
Odette Callingham	**JEN**
Lauren Goodrum	**VAL**
Olivia Dean	**CHRISTINE**

THE CHARACTERS

Lucy Bush	**JACKIE**
Rachel Killington	**JANET**
Chris Lawton	**TREV**
Ben Fox	**CHRISTOPHER**
Daniel Amis	**DAVID**
Caroline Anderson, Matt Ashford, Charis Barwick, Laura Bond, Alice Brown, Chloe Burton, Julie Coleman, Rosy Coppard, Rojo Levien, Harriet Knee, Andrew Martin, Gina Pearce, Catherine Rolfe, Barney Rose, Nikki Shanahan, Anna Sandell, Jo Warner, Tom Wilkins, Emma Yaxley.	**THE CHILDREN OF CLASS 4**
Mandy McKenna, Rob John	**ADULT VOICES**

Directed by Rob John

In 2002 *The Spaceman* was adapted for radio by Rob John. The production, directed by Roland Jaquarello for BBC Radio 4, was first broadcast on 31 January 2003.

ACT 1 ❖ SCENE 1

As the lights go down, we become aware of a black-and-white image projected onto　1
the set. The image is of children playing. A playground scene perhaps. Children
wearing the clothes and haircuts of 1961. We hear piano music in the distance as
Maggie *enters. Like all the children in this play, her costume and hair must look*
exactly like the children in the photograph. ***Maggie*** *stares at the photograph for a*
while, then slowly turns and walks towards the audience. She talks directly to us and,
as she speaks, the music fades and the lights gradually come up on an empty space.
The projected image disappears. The only set is a very long table, which will serve for
mound, benches, school desks and any other structure required by the production.

MAGGIE	When I was eleven, I always wore a green cardigan with red　10 bits on the sleeve. I always had my hair parted like this and fixed on the side with hair grips. *(She shows us.)* When I was eleven, we always used to play up here on Top Field. It's a car park now for Asda but when I was eleven, Top Field was … a field … with a mound of mud you could climb on *(She climbs up onto the table.),* some blackberry bushes and some broken goal posts. The good thing about Top Field was that Michael's house backed onto it and he could see right across it from his bedroom window. I never had to go and call for him. That would have been … well, I couldn't　20 have done that … but if I wanted to play with him, I just had to stand on Top Field and count and before I got to 25, 26, 27, 28, 29. (***Michael*** *sprints on, out of breath.)* Before I got to 30, he'd be there. When I was eleven, Michael was always there.
MICHAEL	Hello, Maggie. What're we doing?
MAGGIE	That Bible thing. Steven's bringing a Bible.
MICHAEL	Right.
	Steven *enters at speed*
STEVEN	Got one!　30

1

MAGGIE	Good. Let's start.
STEVEN	It's an illustrated one though. Got all pictures.
MAGGIE	Doesn't matter.
	Maggie holds the Bible and makes strange hand movements over it. Jen enters. She's also been running fast from somewhere.
JEN	You shouldn't do that … that's the Bible, that is … you shouldn't do that with the Bible.
MICHAEL	Be quiet, Jen.
JEN	That's wrong, that is. You shouldn't do that. Something bad'll happen.
MICHAEL	Shut up, Jen.
STEVEN	It's alright, Jen. Nothing'll happen.
JEN	I'm going home, I am.
STEVEN	It's alright. We're just using the words. Nothing wrong with that. Probably won't even work.
MAGGIE	It'll work.
JEN	Are you sure?
MAGGIE	Yes. Who's going first?
MICHAEL	Me. I'll go first.
MAGGIE	Right. Shut your eyes and think.
MICHAEL	What of?
MAGGIE	Ask it the question.
MICHAEL	Right.
	His mouth moves as he silently asks the question.
MAGGIE	Go on then.
MICHAEL	What?

2

STEVEN	He's scared.
MICHAEL	Shut your gob.
STEVEN	Bog off.
MAGGIE	Quiet ... go on ... just open the Bible ... just let it fall open ... 60 touch the page and read.
	He does.
MAGGIE	What does it say?
MICHAEL	It's a map.
MAGGIE	What?
MICHAEL	It's a map. Joshua's Campaigns in the South.
MAGGIE	Well, that's no good. It can't be a map.
MICHAEL	Well, it is. Look. Joshua's ...
STEVEN	Here. Let me have a go.
	He goes through the ritual, open and points. 70
STEVEN	It's a picture.
MICHAEL	What of?
STEVEN	Some figs ... on a tree.
MICHAEL	How d'you know they're figs?
STEVEN	'Cos it says so. Look. Figs. See? Believe me now?
MAGGIE	It's not working. It's got to be words. You shouldn't have brought the illustrated. Illustrated's no good. Illustrated's for children.
STEVEN	Sorry, Maggie.
MAGGIE	Try again ... Jen? 80
JEN	No ... no. I don't want to. Something bad'll happen.
MAGGIE	Here. Give it here. I'll do it.

She performs an elaborate ritual then points at the open book.

I've got something.

MICHAEL	Words?
MAGGIE	Yeah, words.
STEVEN	Go on then. What's it say?
MAGGIE	*(Reading.)* And darkness was under his feet / And he rode upon a cherub / Yea he did fly upon the wings of the wind.

They all look up, thinking.

ⅽ

STEVEN	What's it mean, Maggie?
MICHAEL	Maggie?
JEN	Are we going to pass our Eleven Plus or not?
MAGGIE	Don't know.
JEN	But you said it would tell us.
STEVEN	You said there'd be a message for us in it. What's it mean?
MAGGIE	I don't know.
STEVEN	I don't know why we listen to you. Why do we always listen to you?

You're mad, you are.

10

He storms out.

JEN	You shouldn't have done that, Maggie. Something bad'll happen to you.

Jen wanders off, looking worried.

MICHAEL	Well that was a waste of time wasn't it?
MAGGIE	No.
MICHAEL	Well, what's it mean then?

MAGGIE	Don't know … but something's going to happen … I'll tell you that for nothing … something's going to happen … it's got to mean something … something big is definitely going to happen … I can feel it.
MICHAEL	Can you?
MAGGIE	Yeah.
	She takes a biscuit out of a brown paper bag and starts to nibble thoughtfully.
MAGGIE	Yeah.
MICHAEL	*(In friendly appreciation rather than romantically.)* I love you, Maggie!
MAGGIE	I'm starting a new club, I am.
MICHAEL	Can I have that biscuit?
MAGGIE	It's not going to be an ordinary club though.
MICHAEL	'Cos, strictly speaking, that biscuit's mine.
MAGGIE	This one's going to be different.
MICHAEL	'Cos we started off this morning with five and you've already had three.
MAGGIE	This one's going to be a secret one. A secret society.
MICHAEL	So, strictly speaking, we should have had two and a half each.
MAGGIE	*(Suddenly shouting.)* Alright, have the biscuit.
MICHAEL	No. Don't want it now.
MAGGIE	Have it.
MICHAEL	No!
	She grabs him by the hair and stuffs the biscuit into his mouth.

110

120

130

MAGGIE	Have it. Have the whole bloody thing, if that's what you want. There. Greedy little git. Enjoying it? Don't know why I put up with you. Don't know why I let you hang round with me. Person who makes a song and dance about a biscuit. Must be nuts. Where are you going?
MICHAEL	Home.
MAGGIE	Why?
MICHAEL	You're not nice to me, Maggie.
MAGGIE	I am ... I am nice to you ... what're you talking about? No, don't go. Michael, don't go ... I'm ... sorry ... shouldn't have done that.
MICHAEL	I could have choked.
MAGGIE	Was only a biscuit.
MICHAEL	I COULD HAVE CHOKED!
MAGGIE	Yeah, you could have. Sorry ... honest ... sorry ... friends?
MICHAEL	Maybe.
	Long pause.
MAGGIE	I'm starting a new club, I am.
MICHAEL	*(Still angry.)* No one'll join.
MAGGIE	Yes, they will.
MICHAEL	People don't like your clubs.
MAGGIE	Yes they do. Everyone joins my clubs.
MICHAEL	Yeah, then they resign 'cos you boss them about and shout at them.
MAGGIE	No, I don't.
MICHAEL	Yes you do. You always do. That's why people resign. 'Cos you shout and scream at them all the time.

14◀

15◀

16◀

MAGGIE	I do not.
MICHAEL	Yes, you do.
MAGGIE	Well, don't join then.
MICHAEL	Don't worry, I won't.
MAGGIE	Good, 'cos I don't need you.
MICHAEL	Good, 'cos I'm not joining.
MAGGIE	Good, 'cos I've asked Steven Bradshaw to be vice-president.
	Pause.
MICHAEL	You haven't!
MAGGIE	I have … and he's agreed.
MICHAEL	He hasn't. You're lying.
MAGGIE	I'm not. He's going to be vice-president and secretary.
MICHAEL	He's not.
MAGGIE	Yes he is. He's coming 'round mine on Saturday to discuss.
MICHAEL	Discuss what?
MAGGIE	Matters.
MICHAEL	Oh.
MAGGIE	Yeah. See.
	Pause.
MICHAEL	So, who else is joining?
MAGGIE	I can't tell you that. It's a secret society, isn't it? Everyone'll have code names. We won't be using people's real names. Everyone'll be known by their code name. For security. And we're having a secret language an' all, so we'll be able to talk to each other and people who aren't in it won't know what we're saying.

170

180

MICHAEL	Oh.
MAGGIE	Yeah.
MICHAEL	I might think about joining then. Give it some thought.
	Pause.
MICHAEL	I could make the badges.
MAGGIE	What badges?
MICHAEL	Your clubs always have badges.
MAGGIE	This is secret. You don't have badges in a secret society.
	Pause.
MICHAEL	Secret badges.
MAGGIE	What?
MICHAEL	I could make secret badges.
MAGGIE	What are secret badges?
MICHAEL	I don't know.
	Pause.
MICHAEL	Are we going to pass, Maggie?
MAGGIE	Course we are. Don't be daft. Course we are. I keep telling you.
MICHAEL	Both of us?
MAGGIE	Of course both of us.
MICHAEL	I love you, Maggie. *(Long pause.)* Do you think the world's going to end? Do you think that's what it means?
MAGGIE	Maybe. Something's going to happen. Something big. Definitely.
MICHAEL	I just hope it's not the end of the world.
MAGGIE	Maybe Jesus'll come back.

19⦁

20⦁

21⦁

MICHAEL	Will he?
MAGGIE	He might. Might have already come back. Might be here now.
MICHAEL	Might have been and gone.
MAGGIE	Maybe the revolution's coming.
MICHAEL	What revolution?
MAGGIE	My dad says there's going to be a revolution.
MICHAEL	When? 220
MAGGIE	I dunno. Some time. Can't tell exactly. But it will happen. It's historically inevitable.
MICHAEL	Oh. What exactly is a revolution, Maggie?
MAGGIE	Well, mainly it means all the millionaires have to share all their money with everyone else.
MICHAEL	Coo. That'll be good.
MAGGIE	Yeah, they have to bring all their money into a big room and place it on the table and then there'd be a box with everybody's name on it, like there'd be a box with your name on it and one with my name on it, and we'd all have 230 our boxes and all the millionaires' money'd be shared out … equally.
MICHAEL	Blimey. What if all the millionaires say, 'No! I'm not sharing. I'm keepin' all my money for myself, I am.'?
MAGGIE	Then we'd have to shoot them.
MICHAEL	Oh.
MAGGIE	We'd give them the choice though. Share. Or be tied up and shot.
MICHAEL	Well, that's fair enough.
MAGGIE	Yeah. 240
MICHAEL	When's all this going to happen then?

MAGGIE	Already has.
MICHAEL	Has it?
MAGGIE	In China, Cuba ... Russia.
MICHAEL	Oh.
MAGGIE	My dad says we have to work tirelessly night and day for the overthrow of the capitalist bourgeois ruling classes in order to establish the dictatorship of the proletariat.
MICHAEL	Oh.
MAGGIE	Yeah.
MICHAEL	That'd be worth it though.
MAGGIE	What'd be worth it?
MICHAEL	That'd be worth working tirelessly night and day for the overthrow of the whatsit if you got a share of the millionaires' money. What size box d'you reckon we'll all get? I reckon it'll be like a shoe box, I do.
MAGGIE	Or maybe there'll just be another war.
MICHAEL	Did you really ask Steven to be in your club?
MAGGIE	Something's going to happen though.
MICHAEL	I think you just made that up, didn't you?
MAGGIE	Something big's definitely going to happen. I can feel it coming.
MICHAEL	I love you, Maggie.
MAGGIE	It's historically inevitable.

25

26

ACT 1 ❖ SCENE 2

*A primary school classroom. Rows of **Children** facing outwards. **Maggie** is in the* 1
front row. The adult characters are heard but not seen.

MISS GREEN	Now stand up, children. The head teacher wants to speak to you.
HEAD TEACHER	Good afternoon, children.
CLASS	Good afternoon, sir.
HEAD TEACHER	This weekend, children ... tomorrow probably ... your parents will receive a letter telling them which school you will attend next year. Now, a lot of time and effort has gone into deciding which is the right school for each and every 10 one of you, and I'm confident that in each case the right decision has been made. So, I don't want to hear on Monday that anybody's been boasting about how clever they were getting into grammar school and I don't want to hear of any tantrums from those who are going to Barton Road. Everyone will be going to the right school and that's all that matters. Understand?
CLASS	Yes, sir.
HEAD TEACHER	Good. Carry on, Miss Green.
MISS GREEN	Now, children, it's nearly home time and there's some very 20 special homework that I'd like you to do over the weekend. Are we all listening? No, I don't think we are, are we Christopher? So, let's put down all our pens and crayons and listen very carefully. That's better. Now, the homework is about something that happened yesterday. Yesterday, something very important happened. Something very special. It happened a long way away, so we didn't hear about it until this morning. Does anybody know what that special thing was?

*The **Children** either look completely vacant or attempt desperately to answer the question by putting up their hands and then withdrawing them.*   **3**

Alright, I'll tell you. Yesterday, the Russians put a man into space.

The class gasp.

Yes, it's true. Yesterday, a man was put inside a space rocket and blasted into space. He travelled right around the world. See this globe, children? He shot up into space from Russia, see here. Then out across the Arctic Circle and over the North Eastern Hemisphere towards the North Pacific. Then,   **4** travelling at 20,000 miles per hour, he crossed over America, Cape Horn and the South Atlantic and then, just as he was sweeping over West Africa, he slowed his engines and he came down from space and landed again in Russia. The whole flight lasted only 108 minutes.

The children have become totally still and silent.

The first man in space. His name is Yuri Gagarin. He'll soon be the most famous man in the whole world. Yuri Gagarin. Look. I've written it on the board. Say it, children. Yuri Gagarin.   **5**

The children repeat the name.

Now what sort of person do you think this Yuri Gagarin is?

A forest of hands go up.

JEN   I think he must be really brave, miss. 'Cos it'd be quite risky going into space because there might not be any air or anything and you could easily die ...

MICHAEL   I think he's clever, miss. 'Cos he'd have to learn to drive the spaceship and it'd probably be quite complicated with lots of dials and knobs and things.

JANET	I think he's quite a small person because they wouldn't pick someone who was really fat or anything 'cos he wouldn't fit in the spaceship ...	60
JACKIE	Or they'd have to make a bigger one ...	
JANET	Yeah ...	
STEVEN	I think he's probably a pilot. A test pilot probably 'cos he'd be trained for flying different kinds of planes.	
CHRISTINE	But it's not a plane. We're not even talking about planes. This is a rocket.	
VAL	I think he's quite a kind person, miss.	
CHRISTOPHER	Why?	70
VAL	I don't know, I just think he is.	
CHRISTOPHER	Why should he be kind? Miss, that's stupid.	
VAL	You're stupid.	
TREV	I think he must be really brave, miss.	
JEN	I said that, miss. I've already said that.	

*A handbell rings. The **Children** start to pack up to go home.*

TEACHER	Alright ... alright, settle down. Now, listen ... listen. We go home when I say so. For homework, I want you all to write a letter to Major Gagarin telling him what you think about his space flight and ... AND ... on Monday, we're going to read out the letters and send them to him in Russia.	80

The class go still again.

Yes. Remember that, children. On Monday your letters are going to Moscow.

Good afternoon, children.

CLASS	Good afternoon, Miss Green.

*The class bustles out except **Maggie**, who has said nothing and sat very still throughout this.*

MICHAEL	You coming, Maggie?
MAGGIE	'And darkness was under his feet / And he rode upon a cherub and did fly / Yea he did fly upon the wings of the wind.' It's him, isn't it?
MICHAEL	Yuri Gagarin?
MAGGIE	Yeah. He did fly upon the wings of the wind. Of course it's him.
MICHAEL	Blimey!

9

ACT 1 ❖ SCENE 3

Christine stands centre stage with her hands over her eyes. In front of her is a new   1
bicycle. Attached to the handlebars is a brown paper parcel. Again, we only hear the
voices of the adults.

FATHER	You can look now, Christine.
	Christine looks.
FATHER	Congratulations, darling.
MOTHER	We're very proud of you.
FATHER	You've done so well.
MOTHER	Go on. Get on it. Try it out.
FATHER	The saddle might need adjusting. 10
MOTHER	Do you like the colour? We thought the blue was right for you.
FATHER	What do you think? A proper grown-up bicycle.
MOTHER	What about the parcel?
FATHER	Open the parcel.
	She does. It's a new school blazer.
MOTHER	Put it on. We ordered it weeks ago. Jumping the gun a bit, I know, but we thought ...
FATHER	We thought ... no, we knew, there'd be good news today. Go on. Put it on. 20
	She does.
MOTHER	Is it too long in the sleeve?
FATHER	She'll grow into it.

MOTHER	Look at her. She looks so grown up.
FATHER	Take a snap. Go on, take one now.
MOTHER	Alright. Look at the camera, darling. Come on. Big smile. Say cheese.

__Christine__ smiles a sickly smile. The camera flashes. Blackout.

ACT 1 ❖ SCENE 4

*Jackie is staring, as if up a staircase. **Janet** joins her.* 1

JACKIE	MUM?
JANET	Has it come?
JACKIE	Dunno. She's got the post up there. MUM! Still in bed. Lazy cow. You had yours?
JANET	Yeah.
JACKIE	Fail?
JANET	No. Passed.
JACKIE	What?
JANET	No. Only joking. Failed. Stupid cow. 10
JACKIE	I was gonna say.
JANET	Had you worried there for a minute, didn't I?
JACKIE	You did.
JANET	No. Failed. Barton Road.
JACKIE	Wish I had mine. Mum, open the post. Going up the rec tonight?
JANET	Dunno. Might. You?
JACKIE	Dunno. Might.
	Long pause.
JANET	Terry thingy goes to Barton Road. 20
JACKIE	Does he?
JANET	Third year.
JACKIE	Yeah? D'you like him?

JANET	No.
JACKIE	You do.
JANET	Don't.
JACKIE	You do.
JANET	I don't.
JACKIE	You do.
JANET	I do not.

Pause.

JACKIE	I do.
JANET	Do you?
JACKIE	Yeah, I do a bit.

*The girls start to giggle. They grab hold of each other's arms and spin round chanting 'Terry! Terry! Terry!' Suddenly, **Janet** breaks off and produces a scrap of newspaper from the sleeve of her cardigan.*

JANET	Here, look at that. Who's that?
JACKIE	I don't know.
JANET	Guess.
JACKIE	I don't know, do I? How am I supposed to know?
JANET	It's him.
JACKIE	Who?
JANET	Yuri Gagarin.
JACKIE	Let's have a look then. Oh yeah. He's alright, isn't he?
JANET	Do you like him?
JACKIE	No.

JANET	You do.	
	Jackie's mum's *voice from upstairs.*	50
MUM	Jackie.	
JACKIE	What?	
MUM	Your thing's come.	
JACKIE	What's it say?	
MUM	Hang about. I'm reading it ... you failed ... Barton Road.	
	Again they spin round giggling and chanting 'Barton Road! Barton Road!'	
JANET	You coming over mine then?	
JACKIE	Alright.	
MUM	Jackie.	60
JACKIE	What?	
MUM	Get me some fags. There's money on the sideboard.	
	The girls completely ignore the request and run off laughing.	

ACT 1 ❖ SCENE 5

Christopher sits at the table fidgeting with the letter, desperate to know its contents.

CHRISTOPHER

Mum, can I open this letter? I think it's my results ... Mum? If you were in space ... you could see right across the world ... it would be completely dark on one side 'cos the sun wouldn't be shining on it but all full of light on the other side ... and the world would turn ... do you think you could see it turning? ... And you could see whole oceans like the Pacific and the Atlantic ... not just bits of oceans but the whole thing ... and sometimes you'd be able to see both poles ... both the Arctic and the Antarctic ... at the same time ... and you could see cloud patterns and storms ... maybe lightning and tornadoes.

Long pause.

Mum, I'm going to open it. This letter ... Mum, I'm opening it.

He opens the letter but doesn't look at it.

I think I'll go into space when I'm older ... yeah, I will definitely go into space when I'm older ...

He shuts his eyes tightly and holds up two sets of crossed fingers. After several seconds, he reads the letter. His face and voice reveal what it says.

Do you think you can see the Earth spinning, Mum? From outer space? ... do you think you can see it turn? ... 'Cos I think I'll ask Yuri Gagarin when I write to him ... he'd know, wouldn't he?

He screws up the letter and hurls it away.

Yeah. He'd know.

ACT 1 ❖ SCENE 6

Maggie and *Michael* *run on from opposite sides.*   1

MICHAEL	Well?
MAGGIE	You go first.
MICHAEL	No, you.
MAGGIE	Alright. I passed.
MICHAEL	I knew it. Knew you would. That's good. Well done, Maggie.
MAGGIE	You?
MICHAEL	I'm pleased for you.
MAGGIE	Michael, tell me.
MICHAEL	Failed. 10
MAGGIE	What?
MICHAEL	I failed.
MAGGIE	You can't have.
MICHAEL	I did.
MAGGIE	You didn't.
MICHAEL	I did.
MAGGIE	You're joking. You're lying.
MICHAEL	Look for yourself if you don't believe me.
	He hands her a letter and she reads.
MAGGIE	Oh bloody bugger. That means … 20
MICHAEL	Barton Road Secondary Modern.
MAGGIE	Oh bloody bugger. I thought we'd … I always thought we'd be going to the grammar together. We had plans. We were going to …

MICHAEL	I let you down, Maggie.
MAGGIE	It's a mistake. They got it wrong. They got you muddled up with someone else. You can appeal. It's a mistake.
MICHAEL	It's not a mistake.
MAGGIE	It's spoilt everything. You stupid little ...
MICHAEL	We can still be friends.
MAGGIE	How can we still be friends? Eh? You don't understand. How can we still be friends? You've spoilt everything. I HATE YOU.

Long pause.

MICHAEL	I've written my letter.
MAGGIE	What?
MICHAEL	I've written my letter to Yuri Gagarin.
MAGGIE	So?
MICHAEL	Do you want to hear it?
MAGGIE	No.
MICHAEL	OK.

Long pause.

MAGGIE	Go on then.
MICHAEL	What?
MAGGIE	Read your letter.
MICHAEL	OK. 'Dear Yuri Gagarin ...'
MAGGIE	How could you do it?
MICHAEL	Do what?
MAGGIE	How could you fail? How could you do that to me?

ACT 1 ❖ SCENE 7

VAL	Did you pass then, Jennifer?	1
JEN	No.	
VAL	Never mind. I'm sure you'll be very happy at Barton Road.	
JEN	Yes.	
VAL	I won't be going to either Barton Road or the grammar.	
JEN	Where you going then?	
VAL	Boarding school ... we haven't decided which one yet ... might be Benenden ... that's the one Princess Anne goes to ... my uncle's paying ... my uncle's really rich ... he's almost a millionaire ...	10
JEN	I'd like to be a millionaire.	
VAL	My uncle's nearly one. He only needs about another £60 and then he'll be one.	
JEN	I like Princess Anne.	
VAL	Yes, she's nice ... I met her last summer ... and she was nice ...	
JEN	Do you think Maggie's going to the grammar?	
VAL	My uncle had a party at his house ... last summer ...	
JEN	I bet she is.	
VAL	He had a party and she came. She wore a green dress and her hair was all like this.	20
	Steven approaches.	
VAL	She had about four servants with her and they have to give her whatever she wants ... if she says get me some cake they have to rush off and get her some.	

STEVEN	Get who some?
VAL	Princess Anne.
JEN	She says she's going to school next year with Princess Anne.
STEVEN	Some people tell lies and you want to smash 'em in the gob. Some people tell lies and you just feel sorry for 'em.
VAL	My uncle's having another party this summer. You can come if you want to.
JEN	Thanks. You pass then, Steven?
STEVEN	Nope.
JEN	Did Maggie pass?
STEVEN	Dunno. Haven't heard.
JEN	I should think she did ... don't you?
STEVEN	Should think so. What about you?
JEN	No. I failed.
STEVEN	Miss Green said I'd passed though. Said I deserved to pass. Said she thought I'd do nicely at the grammar. That's the same as saying I'd passed. Isn't it? I thought it was. Letter comes. Failed. Bloody letter. Bloody Miss Green. I hate her. Telling people they've passed when they haven't.
VAL	He's got this summer house by a lake and they have dances with a real orchestra playing ...
STEVEN	I don't care though. She can go and boil her arse, Miss bloody Green. Who wants to go to the grammar anyway?
JEN	Yeah.
STEVEN	Who wants to go up there?
JEN	I don't.

STEVEN	Stuck-up arseholes, they are.
	Jenny starts to giggle.
STEVEN	Yeah. Great wobbly stuck-up arseholes, they are.
	Jenny practically hysterical.
STEVEN	Yeah, their arses are so stuck-up and wobbly they have to wear special trousers, they do ... their mums have to go down to Spinks' and ask for special wobbly-arsed trousers for grammar school.
	Sound of a bicycle bell. **Christine** *rides in on her new bike.*
CHRISTINE	If anyone so much as touches this bike, I will kill them. Even if you were to accidentally brush your finger against the bell, like this, I would come to your home in the night and kill you. Do you understand?
JEN	Yes.
CHRISTINE	Do you know how much this bike cost?
JEN	No.
CHRISTINE	£9.
JEN	Blimey.
VAL	My uncle's getting me a bike like that 'cept red.
CHRISTINE	Was anyone talking to you?
VAL	No.
CHRISTINE	Then shut up. It's very bad manners to interrupt other people's conversations.
VAL	Sorry.
CHRISTINE	It's a present.
JEN	Your birthday?
CHRISTINE	No, for passing the Eleven Plus, stupid.

60

70

JEN	Oh. Well done.
CHRISTINE	Any of you pass?
JEN	No.
STEVEN	No.
VAL	I've got to go up the shops for my mum.

Valerie sprints off.

CHRISTINE	Yes, 'cos its quite hard to pass the Eleven Plus, isn't it? Not many get through ... but I did ... so I got the bike. Hey, Lesley Martin's dad got her a bike but Lesley failed so they had to take it back. That's ever so funny, that is. Her dad had to take it back. Don't you think that's funny?
JEN	Yeah.
CHRISTINE	But I got mine.
JEN	Good.
CHRISTINE	Listen to that bell, Loud, isn't it? Want to try it?
JEN	No, it's alright.
CHRISTINE	Go on, try it.
JEN	You said you'd kill people if they touched it.
CHRISTINE	I was joking ... stupid.

Jen gingerly rings the bell.

JEN	It's good.

She likes the sound and tries it a few more times.

CHRISTINE	That's enough ... what's the matter with your hair?
JEN	Nothing.
CHRISTINE	Do you ever wash it?
JEN	Yes.

CHRISTINE	Doesn't look like it. What d'you use for shampoo? Fat out of the bottom of the frying pan? Eh? She uses fat for shampoo, she does. What d'you think? I think she gets all the fat out of her mum's frying pan and smears it on her head every morning. What d'you think, Steven?

110

STEVEN	*(Reluctantly.)* Yeah, looks like it.
CHRISTINE	Yeah. Do you hear that? Steven thinks your hair's all covered in fat. Don't you, Steven?
STEVEN	Yeah.
CHRISTINE	I've got to go now. My mum and dad are taking me out for supper. For a proper slap-up, sit-down supper ... to celebrate.
STEVEN	Nice.
CHRISTINE	Gotta go. *(Coming right up to **Jen**.)* See you, fat head.
	She suddenly rings her bell and cycles away. Long pause.
STEVEN	Look, I'm ...

120

JEN	I've written my letter to Yuri Gagarin, I have ...
STEVEN	I'm sorry.
JEN	I've put all about our school and how we're all learning about him.
STEVEN	I'm sorry about what I said then.
JEN	Do you think he'll read all his letters or will someone do it for him, 'cos he might get thousands and it might take ages to read them all?
STEVEN	She makes you say things.
JEN	He'll be the most famous man in the whole world soon but if we can get our letters off first, if we can get ours off on Monday ...

130

STEVEN	She makes you say stupid things.

JEN   Ours might be the first ones he opens and ...

STEVEN   I didn't mean it about your hair.

JEN   ... he might write back.

STEVEN   Your hair's fine.

JEN   Gotta go.

STEVEN   Yeah.

ACT 1 ❖ SCENE 8

Trev sprints on, clutching his letter. He stares intently down the road, waiting for a   1
bus. Janet and Jackie enter, see Trev and start to giggle.

JACKIE	Trev.
TREV	Watcha.
JACKIE	What're you doing?
TREV	Waiting for a bus.
JANET	Where're you going?
TREV	Vera's.
JANET	What're you doing up there?
TREV	Got to take my letter. 10
JACKIE	That your Eleven Plus letter, Trev?
TREV	Yeah. Mum can't read it ... without her glasses. She's broken her glasses. I got to get Vera to tell me what it says. I can't make out all the long words myself.
JACKIE	Did your mum give you the bus fare, Trev?
TREV	Two bob.
JANET	You give us the two bob, Trev, and we'll read the letter for you. Tell you what it says.
JACKIE	Right here, Trev. Save you the trip.
JANET	Whaddya say? 20
TREV	Not sure.
JACKIE	Think about it, Trev. It's going to take you all day to get up there.
JANET	And then your Vera'll probably be out.

JACKIE	And then you'll have to wait for a bus to come back.
JANET	And you still won't know what the letter says.
JANET	Come on, Trev. Give us the two bob and we'll do it now.
TREV	Alright. I suppose.
JACKIE	Gis it here. Right, here we are.
	She makes the sound of a trumpet fanfare.
JACKIE	BARTON ROAD!
	The two girls spin each other round and chant 'Barton Road! Barton Road!'
TREV	Am I going to Barton then?
JANET	Yeah.
TREV	I don't know anyone at Barton.
JACKIE	Yes, you do.
TREV	Do I? Who?
JANET	Us. We're going.
TREV	Are you?
JACKIE	We'll look after you.
TREV	Will you?
JANET	Course we will.
TREV	Thanks.
JANET	That'll be two bob.
TREV	Oh right, yeah. Thanks.

Trev hands over his two bob. The girls exit giggling. Trev looks pleased by the deal then suddenly sprints off.

ACT 1 ❖ SCENE 9

A group of five children including **Maggie, Christine** *and* **David** *stand together.*   1
They are the chosen few. The voice of the **Head teacher** *is heard.*

HEAD TEACHER   Right. Here we are. The Famous Five. I had hoped for a few
more but this hasn't been a vintage year, so there we are.
Right, I'll come straight to the point. I don't believe in
making a big song and dance about the Eleven Plus. You've
passed and the others haven't. You have been chosen and
that means that from now on very high standards are going
to be expected of you. High standards in your work at
school and high standards in your behaviour. Do you   10
understand what I am saying?

THE FIVE   Yes, sir.

HEAD TEACHER   You all proved in the exam that you're clever enough to go
to the grammar school but are you the right material in
other ways? I think you are. I am confident that we have
here five prime examples of the right material. Don't do
anything in the last few weeks to prove me wrong.

THE FIVE   No, sir.

HEAD TEACHER   We once had a girl at this school who got into the grammar
school … got a place … but it went to her head and her   20
behaviour in the last term was so … inappropriate … that we
were forced to advise the grammar school to think again. They
reconsidered her case and her place was withdrawn. It was
reluctantly decided that she was not grammar school material.
But that's not going to happen to you, is it?

THE FIVE   No, sir.

HEAD TEACHER   Of course it's not. Right. That'll be all. Off you go, back to
Miss Green.

        Maggie *remains as the others exit.*

HEAD TEACHER	Yes?
MAGGIE	What did she do?
HEAD TEACHER	Sorry?
MAGGIE	This girl. What did she do wrong?
HEAD TEACHER	That is none of your business, Margaret. Go back to your class.
MAGGIE	Yes. Sorry, sir.

ACT 1 ❖ SCENE 10

The classroom. 1

MAGGIE	Dear Mr Gagarin. On behalf of Class 4 at Howden County Primary School in England, I would like to congratulate you on your achievement …
JEN	Dear Yuri Gagarin, well done for flying into space and not getting killed. It must have been quite scary up there and we all think you are brave and …
CHRISTOPHER	… what I want to know is two things. The first thing is can you see the Earth turning from space? And …
JACKIE	… my best friend, Janet Rigby, thinks you have nice eyes. 10
JANET	I do not. I never said that, miss.
JACKIE	… and she said she'd like to …
JANET	… I would not. She's making it up, miss …
DAVID	I wonder which was the most dangerous part of the flight? I thought at first it might be the take-off because they would have to ignite all that fuel to blast you into space but …
CHRISTOPHER	… secondly, what colour is space when you are in it? Is it black or blue like the sky and another thing is …
MAGGIE	… in our class we are doing a project about you and our teacher, Miss Green, has put a picture of you on the wall and … 20
TREV	… I have got two cats a dog and a hamster called Bob and …
VAL	… my uncle used to be a test pilot and so he knows a lot about flying and so he can get me lots of information about space which an ordinary pupil would be unable to obtain.

CHRISTINE	I expect you will get hundreds of letters and you won't have time to read them all and anyway I'm not sure that you can speak English.
DAVID	... but then I read about the high temperatures which are produced as the rocket re-enters the Earth's atmosphere ...
STEVEN	... and did you have to do much training for the flight and do you actually have to fly the rocket like a plane or do you just sit there because ...
TREV	... yesterday it rained ...
STEVEN	... I read they sent a dog into space and a dog could not fly a rocket, even with special training.
TREV	... but today it is sunny ...
CHRISTINE	... so I told Miss Green that I didn't think there was much point in writing to you ...
MICHAEL	... because the revolution which, as you know, took place in your country in 1917 was a good idea because all the millionaires had to share out their money with the poorer people and I think that this is good and I may myself decide to work tirelessly night and day for the overthrow of the ...
MAGGIE	... and we have enjoyed learning about you and your flight and we have seen your picture in the papers and on TV. If ever you come to England, we would all like to meet you and shake your hand because we think you are so brave. Yours sincerely, your Friends in Class 4.
TREV	PS I have drawn you a picture of some spiders.

3

4

5

ACT 1 ❖ SCENE 11

*The classroom. The **Children** are listening intently, following the conversing voices* 1
as they would a tennis match.

MISS GREEN	Children. Stand up for the head teacher, please.
HEAD TEACHER	So we've been writing to the spaceman, have we Miss Green?
MISS GREEN	Yes. All the children have written.
HEAD TEACHER	So I hear. And what are we planning to do with these letters, Miss Green?
MISS GREEN	We're going to send them to him.
HEAD TEACHER	Actually send them to him in Russia?
MISS GREEN	Yes.
HEAD TEACHER	I think not, Miss Green.
MISS GREEN	*(A little confused.)* Oh. Right.
HEAD TEACHER	Yes, I think writing them is fine as far as it goes. Absolutely fine to write the letters as an imaginative exercise but to actually send them … I think perhaps not.
MISS GREEN	I see. Well perhaps we'll just stick them into our exercise books.
HEAD TEACHER	Yes, that would be more appropriate in this instance. Carry on, Miss Green.

*   **Maggie** puts her hand up.*   20

MAGGIE	Excuse me, sir.
HEAD TEACHER	Yes?
MAGGIE	Why aren't we going to send the letters, sir?

HEAD TEACHER	It wouldn't be appropriate, Maggie.
MAGGIE	Why? Why not? They're good letters. We asked him lots of good questions. They're good letters. You haven't even read them. Everybody tried really hard. You haven't even read them. It's not fair.
HEAD TEACHER	Now you listen to me, Margaret Bailey. You may think you're a very grown up young lady, and I'm sure that you're going to make a very big impression at the grammar school, but there are a lot of things you don't know about the world. Let me tell you something. Your friend Mr Gagarin is a Russian, isn't he? Except they don't call themselves Russians any more, do they? They call themselves Soviets, don't they? The Soviet Union … the Union of Soviet Socialist Republics or whatever … and they call themselves that because they are communists. Now I'll tell you three things about communists, children. They don't believe in God, they don't believe in freedom, and they certainly don't believe in telling the truth. How do we know that your Yuri Gagarin actually went into space? Eh? How do we know he even did it? We've only got their word for it. And do we trust them? Well, you might, Margaret Bailey, but I'm afraid I do not. There'll be no letters to Russia from this school. Understand? UNDERSTAND?
CLASS	Yes, sir.
HEAD TEACHER	Good. Carry on, Miss Green.
MISS GREEN	I'm sorry, Class 4. I didn't realise that Mr Andrews felt so strongly. I'm sure he's right though. I'm sure it's best we don't actually send the letters. I'm sorry if you're disappointed.
	A hand bell sounds.
MISS GREEN	I'll see you all tomorrow. Good afternoon, children.
CLASS	Good afternoon, Miss Green.

*The children watch **Miss Green** leave the room and then slowly start to pack up. **Maggie** hasn't moved.*

MAGGIE How much d'you reckon it'd cost to send a letter to Moscow?

*The **Children** stop packing up.*   60

MICHAEL You're not going to send your letter … are you?

MAGGIE Why not? Why not send them all? Look I've got an envelope. Who's in? Who wants to write to Yuri?

JEN We can't.

MAGGIE Why not?

JEN Mr Andrews said we mustn't.

VAL He'll go mad.

CHRISTINE You'll get into really big trouble.

CHRISTOPHER He'll find out. He's bound to find out.

MAGGIE Who cares? Who cares if he finds out? He can't stop us. It's   70
a free country. We are free to write to anyone. Anyone, anywhere in the world. He can't stop us. Look. This is my envelope. It's mine. I'm putting my letter inside it. Look, I'll put my address on it. The school'll never find out.

JACKIE He said they were bad people. He said we shouldn't write to communists.

JANET He said Yuri didn't even do it.

MAGGIE Yuri did it!

CHRISTINE How do you know?

MAGGIE I just know. I just know he did it. He flew in space. He did   80
fly upon the wings of the wind. It really happened. (*Long pause.*) I'm sending him my letter. Anybody else?

TREV He's a real spaceman, right Maggie?

MAGGIE	Yeah, Trev. He's a real spaceman
TREV	Then I'm sending him mine.
MAGGIE	Thanks. Anyone else?
STEVEN	Oh, why not? Andrews is an arsehole anyway. Probably doesn't even believe in God himself.
VAL	Yeah, why not?

*The **Children** crowd forward to hand their letters to **Maggie**.* 9
* **Christine** stands back.*

MAGGIE	Christine?
CHRISTINE	He won't read them.
MAGGIE	Yes, he will.
CHRISTINE	You don't even know his address.
MAGGIE	Yes, I do. Look.

***Maggie** writes on the envelope.*

MAGGIE	'Yuri Gagarin … Spaceman … Russia.' There won't be two of them, will there? You in?
CHRISTINE	Oh, go on then. 10
MAGGIE	This is the start of a club. A new club. It's going to be called … the Yuri Gagarin club.
JACKIE	Fan club.
JANET	Yeah, fan club's better.
JACKIE	'Cos we're like his fans, aren't we?
MAGGIE	Yeah, I suppose so … and it's going to be a secret club.
CHRISTINE	Why?
MICHAEL	'Cos if Andrews finds out, he'll go mental.
STEVEN	Yeah … yeah … so nobody says nothing about it, right? … Or else.

JEN	So, what do we do in this club?	110
MAGGIE	We follow Yuri. We find out about him. Yeah, if there's something about him in the paper, we cut it out and collect it …	
MICHAEL	… and stick it in a book.	
MAGGIE	Yeah, a secret scrap book.	
MICHAEL	And no one'll know about it, 'cept us.	
MAGGIE	And we'll have a secret language an' all. With secret words like …	
DAVID	Da svidaniya.	
	They all turn and stare at him.	120
MAGGIE	What?	
DAVID	Da svidaniya. It's Russian. It means goodbye.	
STEVEN	How d'you know that?	
DAVID	My brother. He's got this 'Teach Yourself Russian' book. Phrasebook type of thing. I borrowed it.	
STEVEN	What … you taught yourself Russian?	
DAVID	No. Just da svidaniya. I just taught myself da svidaniya. That's as far as I got.	
MAGGIE	That's it. That could be our secret language. We'll teach ourselves Russian. Can you get hold of the book?	130
DAVID	Think so.	
MAGGIE	Bring it in tomorrow. Right. Everyone who wants to join the club, put your hand up.	
MICHAEL	You have to promise to work tirelessly night and day to serve the club.	
JEN	I can't work tirelessly night and day on Wednesdays. I got Brownies.	

MAGGIE	Yeah alright, Jen. Right, everyone who wants to join has to lick the envelope.
	The envelope is passed round and solemnly licked. 14
CHRISTINE	I'm not licking that!
MAGGIE	Then don't. Don't join.
CHRISTINE	Oh, alright. You're all mad, you are.
	Christine *shuts her eyes and licks.* **Maggie** *seals the envelope and holds it up. Faint sound of the Soviet National Anthem, as if in the distance.*
MAGGIE	Goodbye letters. Da svidaniya!
CLASS	Da svidaniya!
MAGGIE	To the spaceman.
CLASS	To the spaceman. 15
	The music swells. Blackout.

ACT 2 ❖ SCENE 1

CHRISTOPHER	This is stupid. What're we doing this for?	1
STEVEN	Maggie said we had to cut out the pictures.	
CHRISTOPHER	So what? Why do we always have to do what she says?	
STEVEN	'Cos it's a good idea.	
CHRISTOPHER	Why? Why is it a good idea?	
STEVEN	Because …	
MICHAEL	Because we're going to have the biggest collection of Yuri Gagarin stuff in England and they're all going to be stuck in this book.	
STEVEN	The Yuri Gagarin fan club scrap book. *(He holds it up.)*	10
MICHAEL	And we're going to give it to him.	
CHRISTOPHER	How are we going to give it to him?	
MICHAEL	When he comes … to visit. When he comes to England.	
CHRISTOPHER	Well, that's stupid, that is.	
STEVEN	Why is it?	
CHRISTOPHER	Well, he won't want pictures of himself. What would he do with pictures of himself?	
STEVEN	Show people. Show them to his children.	
CHRISTOPHER	He hasn't got any children, has he?	
MICHAEL	David?	20
DAVID	*(Checks Yuri fact file.)* One. Baby girl. Natasha. Born October 1960.	
STEVEN	See? Natasha'll probably be really glad to see all these pictures of her dad … one day.	
CHRISTOPHER	I think it would be better to give him something more useful.	

MICHAEL	Like what?
CHRISTOPHER	A jumper.
MICHAEL	A what?
CHRISTOPHER	*(Confidentially.)* Look, my aunt has got this machine. A machine that knits, right? A knitting machine. And you can do patterns on it. She's done me one with a sailing dinghy on the front. It's really lovely. The thing is, I bet I could get her to do one for him *(Dramatic pause.)* … with a rocket on it.
STEVEN	What, a space rocket?
CHRISTOPHER	No, a bloody firework. Of course a space rocket.
MICHAEL	A space rocket on a jumper?
CHRISTOPHER	Yeah.
STEVEN	Well, he's going to love that, isn't he? I bet he can't wait to hang up his uniform and get himself into one of your aunt's homemade jumpers.
CHRISTOPHER	Alright, it was just an idea.
STEVEN	I can just see Yuri shaking hands with the Queen wearing a jumper with a bloody rocket on the front.
CHRISTOPHER	Forget it.
STEVEN	Course, when the Queen sees it, she's going to want one too.
CHRISTOPHER	*(Shouting.)* Shut yer gob, you.
	Long pause.
STEVEN	She could have a line of little corgis going up her sleeves.
	Christopher jumps on **Steven**. *They fight.* **Michael** *and* **David** *break it up.* **Trev** *carries on snipping.*
TREV	Got one! *(Holds up picture.)* Got one of Yuri!
MICHAEL	That's Bobby Charlton, Trev.
TREV	Is it? Oh right.

Margin numbers: 3, 4, 5

ACT 2 ❖ SCENE 2

MAGGIE	It won't make any difference. Honestly, Michael. Everything'll be the same. We can still be together … Saturdays … Sundays … evenings. So, what's changed? … Nothing … I'll be wearing a blue blazer and you'll get a green one, that's all. Apart from that, everything's the same … oh, come on, Michael. We're still friends. We're still us … aren't we? Everything'll just carry on as normal.	1
MICHAEL	Will it?	
MAGGIE	Yes.	
MICHAEL	Doesn't feel like it. Feels like the end of everything.	10
MAGGIE	No, it's the start. Everything's just beginning.	
MICHAEL	When my brother passed … when we got the letter, my dad, he hugged him and he said he was the proudest dad in the whole world. When my letter came … he just hugged me. Didn't say anything. Didn't know what to say, did he?	
MAGGIE	It doesn't matter, Michael.	
MICHAEL	Yes it does. It does matter. It bloody matters. My brother … my brother plays rugby … and he does Latin and Greek and German, and he plays the clarinet in the school orchestra and he's going on the French exchange. He might even go to university and you know what I'm going to get? I'm going to get football and metalwork and technical drawing every day. That's all they do.	20
MAGGIE	They do other things, Michael.	
MICHAEL	No, they do not. You have to do them all day. That's all they do.	
MAGGIE	You don't want to learn Latin.	
MICHAEL	How do you know?	

MAGGIE	It's a dead language.
MICHAEL	So? So what. I might want to learn it. What if I want to learn it?
MAGGIE	I'll teach you.
MICHAEL	You'll teach me Latin?
MAGGIE	Yeah, why not?
MICHAEL	Don't be stupid.
MAGGIE	I can, I will.
MICHAEL	You don't see it, do you? I'm not supposed to learn it. They don't want me to learn it. I haven't been chosen to learn it ... it's another bloody secret language, innit?
	He slopes off.
MAGGIE	Michael, don't go ... oh, Michael, don't go ... look, I won't go to the grammar.
	Michael *stops and looks at her.*
MAGGIE	I'll write and tell them ... I'm not bothered about the grammar. Doesn't matter to me ... I'll go to Barton ... with you.
	Long pause. He stares at her before walking off. **Val** *and* **Jen** *arrive.*
JEN	Look, Maggie. Look what I've found.
MAGGIE	What?
JEN	Photos. Lots of photos.
MAGGIE	(*Not interested.*) Yeah?
JEN	No, look who they're of. Yuri.
MAGGIE	Nice.
JEN	They were in my mum's magazine. I cut 'em out. She doesn't know.

MAGGIE	Oh.
JEN	Is something wrong?
MAGGIE	What?
JEN	Aren't we doing this any more?
MAGGIE	Doing what?
JEN	You said we should collect everything we could about Yuri.
MAGGIE	Oh, yeah.
JEN	You said we were going to paste them in a special book and give it to him when he comes.
MAGGIE	If he comes.
JEN	But you said he'd come. You said one day he'd come to England.
MAGGIE	Yeah. He will. He will come.
JEN	So we've got to be ready for him, haven't we?
MAGGIE	Yeah … yeah, that's right.
JEN	So, do you want these pictures or not?
MAGGIE	Yeah, of course we do. Well done, Jen.
	Maggie *and* ***Jen*** *exit.*
VAL	*(Calling after them.)* I've got some big photos of Yuri. In colour. They're about this big. No, bigger than that. About this big. AND I'M BRINGING THEM IN TOMORROW.

60

70

ACT 2 ❖ SCENE 3

*The **Yuri fan club** has grown. **Steven** moves around the assembled members handing out bits of paper.*

STEVEN	Right. Listen. You've got to learn these.
MICHAEL	Off by heart.
STEVEN	Yeah. And when you've learnt them, destroy the evidence.
MICHAEL	Immediately.
STEVEN	Like this.
	Puts a piece of paper in his mouth eats, tries to swallow, fails and puts it soggily in his pocket.
CHRISTOPHER	What do these words mean?
STEVEN	They're the days of the week … in Russian.
CHRISTOPHER	What do we need the days of the week for?
STEVEN	I dunno. Maggie said we had to learn them.
MICHAEL	Meetings.
CHRISTOPHER	What?
MICHAEL	Say we were planning a meeting and we didn't want anyone to know when it was we'd just say … there a meeting on Pyatnitsa.
JANET	What?
DAVID	Friday.
MICHAEL	Exactly. Friday – Pyatnitsa.
JANET	That's good that is.
MICHAEL	So any questions? Good. So, these are your secret code names.
	He gives out more bits of paper.

10

20

STEVEN	Learn them and dispose of them like this.
	Thinks about previous disposal attempt and tears a piece of paper up.
TREV	What's mine say?
MICHAEL	Yours says 'Tri'. It's the number three in Russian.
TREV	I don't get it.
STEVEN	You're number three, Trev. Tri, Trev. Should be easy to remember.
TREV	Right. Tri.
MICHAEL	Good, Trev. Well done.
TREV	Tri.
MICHAEL	Yeah. Right, who's not here?
TREV	Tri.
MICHAEL	Alright, Trev. Who's not here?
JACKIE	Maggie.
MICHAEL	Well she's number one. Adin.
JEN	And Christine?
STEVEN	Oh, bloody Christine. Give her a difficult one.
JEN	Yeah give her thirty-six-and-a-half or something.
STEVEN	Yeah give her 42,329,612-and-a-half. Take her about a year to learn it. Or give her something rude. Give her something rude in Russian.
	They stop and stare at each other.
STEVEN	Shall we?
MICHAEL	She'd go mad.
JEN	She'd kill us.
STEVEN	She'll never know, will she? David, what've you got?

30

40

50

47

DAVID	It's just a phrase book. Hasn't got rude words. Hang about, 'At the Doctor's'. There's a section on what to say if you get ill.
STEVEN	Gimme … got it … panos … diarrhoea!
JEN	We can't. We'll never get away with it.
MICHAEL	Quick. Write it down.
JACKIE	She's coming.
	Christine *enters.*
MICHAEL	You're late.
CHRISTINE	So?
MICHAEL	We're giving out numbers in Russian.
STEVEN	Secret code numbers.
MICHAEL	This is yours.
STEVEN	You have to learn it … off by heart.
MICHAEL	You're number six. Panos.
	The others just about manage to stifle giggles.
CHRISTINE	This is really stupid.
MICHAEL	Look, do you want to be in this or not?
CHRISTINE	Oh, go on then.
MICHAEL	Got it?
CHRISTINE	Yes.
MICHAEL	Learnt it?
CHRISTINE	Yes, I'm not stupid.
MICHAEL	Alright then, let's practise. So Maggie's adin, I'm dva. Trev?
TREV	*(Triumphantly.)* Tri.

6

7

STEVEN	Well done, Trev.
MICHAEL	Jackie?
JACKIE	Chetyre.
MICHAEL	David?
DAVID	Pyat.
MICHAEL	Christine?
CHRISTINE	Panos.
STEVEN	Hang about. What did you say you were?
CHRISTINE	Panos.
STEVEN	I thought I was panos.
CHRISTINE	No, I'm panos.
STEVEN	Are you sure?
CHRISTINE	Course I'm sure. I am panos. It says so on my piece of paper. Look, panos.
STEVEN	Oh yeah. Yeah, you are panos, aren't you? Sorry. My mistake. Panos.

By this stage they can't control the laughter any more.

CHRISTINE	Why's everybody laughing?

They all go very still and quiet and scared.

CHRISTINE	It means something else, doesn't it? What's it mean? What's it mean? Valerie, tell me what it means or I'll tell them what you keep in your shoulder bag.
VAL	No don't. Don't say. Please.
CHRISTINE	Then tell me.
VAL	Diarrhoea.
CHRISTINE	What?

80

90

100

VAL	Means diarrhoea.
CHRISTINE	You're pathetic. All of you. You're so childish. You make me sick. I don't want to be in this club anyway. I resign. And by the way, she keeps dry knickers in her shoulder bag 'cos she never knows when she might need to change, do you Val?

*Embarrassed silence. **Val** is in tears.*

MICHAEL	That wasn't very nice, was it?	
CHRISTINE	Wasn't very nice what you did to me, was it?	
MICHAEL	Sorry.	11
STEVEN	Sorry.	

***Maggie** enters.*

MAGGIE	Right, listen. Listen to this, everyone. What's the matter? What's happened?	
MICHAEL	Nothing.	
MAGGIE	Look!	
CHRISTINE	What is it?	
MAGGIE	A letter.	
CHRISTINE	I can see that. What letter?	
MAGGIE	A letter from him. From Yuri.	12

Gasps

TREV	What … Yuri's written back?
MAGGIE	Yes, he's written back.
CHRISTOPHER	What, really?
MAGGIE	Yes. Look!
CHRISTOPHER	Blimey!
JEN	What's he say?

CHRISTOPHER	Did he answer our questions?	
STEVEN	Can he speak English?	
TREV	Did he like my drawings?	130
JACKIE	Read it. Go on, read it.	
MAGGIE	'USSR Cosmonaut Major Yuri Alexeyevich Gagarin thanks you for your kind wishes expressed on the occasion of his historic flight into space on 12th April 1961. Comrade Major Gagarin is looking forward to meeting his many friends in Great Britain when he visits your country in the near future.'	
CHRISTOPHER	Blimey. He is coming.	
JACKIE	He's looking forward to meeting his many friends.	
JANET	That's us, isn't it Maggie? His many friends in Great Britain. That's us.	140
JEN	When's he coming, Maggie?	
MAGGIE	Doesn't say.	
JEN	He could come at any time.	
MAGGIE	That's right. We've got to be ready.	
JEN	He might come next week.	
STEVEN	And the scrap book's not ready yet. We've got to get more stuff.	
CHRISTINE	This is stupid this is. He didn't even write it himself. *(The group are outraged by this suggestion.)* Well he didn't, did he? It doesn't say 'my many friends', it says, 'his many friends'. It's obvious HE never wrote that. Someone wrote it for him.	150
JEN	Maggie?	
MAGGIE	It's the way they write. In Russia. They don't say 'I' in Russia. Unless they have to. It's rude to talk about yourself in Russia. You have to talk about yourself as if you were someone else.	

CHRISTINE	Why?
MAGGIE	'Cos … 'cos they're communists.
MICHAEL	Yeah, it's part of overthrowing the capitalist bourgeois ruling classes.
CHRISTINE	I still don't think he wrote it himself. He never even signed it.
MAGGIE	No, but he signed this.
	She produces a signed photo of Yuri.
JAN	His photograph. He's sent a signed photograph.
CHRISTOPHER	He's really signed it. You can see where the pen's dented the paper. It's real.
JEN	He's really signed it.
VAL	I think he's signed it 'specially for us.
JACKIE	Definitely.
JANET	He's lovely, isn't he? Well, he is!
JACKIE	Yeah, he is. He's lovely.
VAL	You feel like you sort of know him, don't you?
JEN	Yeah. You do.
MAGGIE	*(To **Christine**.)* Want a look?
CHRISTINE	No, I don't actually. I think you've gone mad actually. He's a Russian. Russians are worse than Germans. My dad says so. He says Russians are worse than the Nazis. My dad says the Russians are planning to take over the whole world and turn everybody into communists and, if they don't get their way, they'll blow everything up with atom bombs. They're evil, Russians are. Evil barbarians. So I don't want to take a look at your precious picture, thank you very much, and I don't want to be in your stupid club any more either. I resign.

16

17

18

MAGGIE	*(Very calm and right up close to **Christine**.)* Well, I'm heartbroken.
CHRISTINE	You make me sick, you do.
MAGGIE	Then I should keep well out of my way if I were you.
CHRISTINE	You better watch it.
MAGGIE	Watch what?
CHRISTINE	I could tell on you. I could tell Mr Andrews.
MAGGIE	Tell him what?
CHRISTINE	That you're doing all this Russian stuff. He'll go mad, he will. You'll be in really big trouble, you will. So, you be careful what you say to me … all of you. Just be careful.
	She storms off.
MAGGIE	*(Shouting after her.)* I'm not scared of you. I'M NOT SCARED OF YOU.
JEN	*(Coming up to **Maggie** and holding her hand.)* You're not scared of anybody, are you Maggie?

190

200

ACT 2 ❖ SCENE 4

JEN	Do you love her?
MICHAEL	Love who?
JEN	Maggie.
MICHAEL	No.
JEN	You do.
MICHAEL	No, I don't.
JEN	You spend a lot of time with her.
MICHAEL	So? ... So what? ... A person can spend a lot of time with someone without loving 'em.
VAL	I was in love with someone once.
JEN	I like Maggie.
MICHAEL	Do you?
JEN	She's clever, isn't she?
MICHAEL	Suppose so.
VAL	He was in love with me too.
JEN	She has all these plans. She always knows what to do next. I can never think of what to do next, me.
VAL	We were going to get married.
JEN	Sometimes I pretend that she's my sister. That we're sort of like twins, me and Maggie.
MICHAEL	Why? What for?
JEN	Don't know. Just do. I wish she was my sister. You won't tell her, will you?

1

2

MICHAEL	No.
VAL	He moved away.
MICHAEL	Who moved away?
VAL	This boy.
MICHAEL	Which boy?
VAL	This boy I was going to get married to. He moved away to America. Or India … can't remember. But he definitely moved away.
JEN	D'you think we'll see Maggie when she goes to the grammar?
MICHAEL	Yeah. *(Pause.)* Yeah.
JEN	D'you think we'll all still meet up and everything?
MICHAEL	Yeah. Course we will.
JEN	D'you think we'll still have the Yuri fan club?
MICHAEL	What are you talking about? What's the matter with you?
JEN	I just worry that when she goes to the grammar, she won't want us any more.
	Pause.
MICHAEL	I gotta go.
	***Michael** exits*
VAL	So, that was the end of that.
JEN	End of what?
VAL	Me and this boy.

30

40

ACT 2 ❖ SCENE 5

*The **Yuri Fan Club** look expectantly at **Maggie**.*

MAGGIE	Right, put the box on the table, David. We've all got to put our facts in this box. Put your hand up if you haven't got a fact.
	One kid hasn't.
STEVEN	Why not?
KID 1	I couldn't get one.
STEVEN	Didn't you understand. Didn't we make it clear? You had to bring a fact.
KID 1	I couldn't get any facts.
STEVEN	How many facts you get, Trev?
TREV	Fourteen.
STEVEN	See? If even Trev can get … how many?
TREV	Fourteen.
STEVEN	You got fourteen facts?
TREV	Yeah.
STEVEN	See? Trev can get fourteen facts and you can't even manage to get one measly fact.
KID 1	Sorry.
STEVEN	I should think so too. You need to think very seriously about your attitude you do if you want to stay in this club.
JEN	She can have one of mine.
STEVEN	What?
JEN	I got three facts and she can have one if she wants. There.

1

2

KID 1	Thanks.
STEVEN	You're lucky this time. Don't let it happen again.
KID 1	Sorry.
MAGGIE	Right. Right, you've got to come up tell what your fact is and then put it in the box.
MICHAEL	The Yuri fact box.
MAGGIE	Yeah.

*Hands go up. **Maggie** indicates a child who then comes up, reads, folds a piece of paper and puts it in the box.*

KID 2	Yuri's wife is called Valentina but he calls her Valya for short.
MAGGIE	Good. Good fact. Pop it in.
KID 3	The first person to meet Yuri when he came down from space was a tractor driver called Yakov Lysenko.
MAGGIE	Yeah, good. Trev?
TREV	Yuri has got a dog called Coco.
MAGGIE	Well done, Trev. Good fact. Steven.
STEVEN	As the rocket took off, Yuri shouted out … hang about I've got it here … he shouted out 'Poyekhali!' which means 'Off we go!'
MAGGIE	Poyekhali! That's good. We can use that. Poyekhali!
CLASS	Poyekhali!
KID 4	Yuri was born on 9th March 1934.
KID 5	Yuri's rocket took off at six minutes past nine … in the morning.
TREV	Yuri has not got any cats.
KID 6	Yuri has got two brothers and a sister. The sister is called Zoya. I don't know what the brothers are called.

30

40

50

KID 7	I do. I got that one. *(Reads.)* His two brothers are called Valentin and Boris.
KID 8	When Yuri took off, he was a senior lieutenant but, by the time he'd landed 108 minutes later, they had made him a major. That's higher up.
TREV	Yuri has not got any fish.
MICHAEL	Are all your facts like this, Trev?
TREV	What d'you mean?
MICHAEL	Are all your other facts about Yuri not having pets?
TREV	Yeah.
STEVEN	Well, that's not very good, is it?
TREV	I had to do that 'cos he's only got one pet. You said we had to get as many facts as we could.
STEVEN	You can't do that. He can't do that. Not having fish isn't a fact.
MICHAEL	It's alright, Trev. Put all your facts in together.
	Trev *puts them into the box.*
MAGGIE	Next. Alright, Valerie.
VAL	When he was up there, in space, the controllers on the ground were talking to him on the radio and they asked *(Puts on posh voice.)* 'What is it like up there, Yuri? What can you see?' And Yuri said, 'I can see everything. And it's beautiful.'
STEVEN	She's making it up, she is. She's not allowed to put made-up stuff in the fact box.
MICHAEL	No. She's not making it up. It's my fact too. I GOT THE SAME ONE. They said, 'What can you see?' and he said, 'I can see everything and it's beautiful.'

ACT 2 ❖ SCENE 6

JEN	What'll it be like when we get to London, Maggie? Tell us again.	1
MAGGIE	Well, we get off the train … at the station.	
DAVID	Liverpool Street.	
MAGGIE	Yeah, Liverpool Street.	
JEN	Have you been there before, Maggie?	
VAL	I have. I've been to London hundreds of times. We go almost every holiday. I've been to the Houses of Parliament and Westminster Abbey and the Zoo and the Tower …	
	***Val** continues to list places to herself as **Maggie** carries on.*	10
MAGGIE	Then we'll ask a policeman the way to Earl's Court.	
JACKIE	What's Earl's Court?	
MAGGIE	It's a big sort of castle thing. It's where all the Dukes and Earls go. They have all these big ceremonies there. Courtly things. It's where they're going to take Yuri when he arrives. It was in the papers.	
JAN	Is it far from the station?	
STEVEN	Yeah, 'cos we've got all this Yuri clobber to carry.	
MAGGIE	No, it's probably just round the corner. Probably about a five-minute walk from Liverpool Street.	20
JACKIE	Then what do we do?	
MAGGIE	Well, we get there early, right. And we find a spot near the steps.	
JACKIE	What steps?	
MAGGIE	There'll be steps. There's bound to be steps. Steps for him to walk up.	

JACKIE	Right.
MAGGIE	So, if the steps are here. We'll be here.
	Maggie gets them into position.
MAGGIE	And we'll have our Yuri scrap book.
MICHAEL	And the fact box.
JEN	And the flags.
STEVEN	And the banner.
MAGGIE	And we'll be ready. And the sun'll be shining. It'll be a beautiful day. It'll be hot but we'll be OK because there'll be a bloke selling ice creams just here. Um, I'll have a lemon lolly, please …
	They all start buying imaginary ice creams off an imaginary ice-cream man. Some of them actually seem to believe in the whole fiction of the moment, calling out things like 'Get me a Mivvi' and 'Can I have a flake in mine?'
MICHAEL	Suddenly a fat bloke barges in front of us and we can't see.
	General horror and outrage.
MICHAEL	But it's alright 'cos a nice policeman says, 'Oi, move yourself. These kids can't see.'
STEVEN	Yeah, get out the way, fatty.
	They 'watch' the fat bloke move.
MAGGIE	And then, in the distance, we can see Yuri's car coming round the corner.
MICHAEL	It's a big black one.
DAVID	A Bentley.
MAGGIE	And there's motorcycle policemen on either side.
JEN	To protect Yuri from the crowds …

MAGGIE	… who are pressing forward and cheering. The car comes closer and starts to slow down.
VAL	I can see him! I can see Yuri!
TREV	Where?
VAL	In the car. In the back of the car.
TREV	Oh yeah. Yuri! Yuri! Hey, Yuri, it's me, Trev!
MAGGIE	The car stops … just here and a policeman opens the rear door and … out steps … Yuri.

                      60

There's total stillness as they 'see' Yuri. The whole scene goes into slow motion for a moment.

MAGGIE	He walks past us. He hasn't seen us. He's about to go up the steps.
JEN	Quick, Maggie, do something. Shout out to him. Quickly!
MAGGIE	Suddenly, I shout out 'Yuri!' And we hold up our stuff.

They hold up banner, pictures of Yuri, the fact box, the scrap book, flags etc.

MICHAEL	And he stops in his tracks …
CHRISTOPHER	… and he turns and looks in our direction …

                      70

VAL	… he looks surprised but then he smiles …
JANET	He's got a lovely smile.
JACKIE	And then suddenly …
JEN	… he's walking towards us!
JANET	Oh my God, he's walking towards us!
VAL	I gotta go to the toilet.
MAGGIE	And he comes right up to us and I say, 'Tovarish Yuri Alexeyevich, dobroe utro.'
ALL	Dobroe utro, Yuri.

MAGGIE	Kak vy pozhivaete? (How are you?) Ochin priyatna paznakomitsa. (I'm pleased to meet you).
MICHAEL	And we show him the scrap book.
STEVEN	And the banner.
DAVID	And the fact box.
JANET	And he looks at the pictures of himself ...
JACKIE	... and he smiles ...
JEN	... and he knows who we are 'cos he remembers our letters ...
CHRISTOPHER	... and he says thanks for being his fans. Says he really appreciates it ... 'cept in Russian, of course.
STEVEN	And he says he hopes we'll keep in touch.
MAGGIE	And there's hundreds of photographers and they ask Yuri if they can take a picture of him with us and he says yes, so they do.
	They pose for photographs with Yuri.
MAGGIE	And he's shaking our hands. And then he's up the steps and gone. Da svidaniya, Yuri Alexeyevich.
ALL	*Da svidaniya!*
	*They slowly disperse, leaving just **Trev** and **Michael**.*
TREV	*(A bit puzzled.)* We were making that up, right?
MICHAEL	Yeah, Trev. Just pretending.
TREV	*(Nods.)* Right.

1

ACT 2 ❖ SCENE 7

MAGGIE   Right, ticket money. David?   1

DAVID   Malcolm still owes three and six.

MALCOLM   I'll pay Saturday, Maggie.

MAGGIE   I've told you. We've got to have the money now. He could come at any time. They could announce it today. He could be here any minute. We've got to be ready.

MALCOLM   Please Maggie. Give me 'til Saturday.

MAGGIE   Alright. 'Til Saturday. But I'm warning you. You don't pay, you're not going.

DAVID   Christopher still owes two bob.   10

CHRISTOPHER   I've got it here.

Christopher hands the money to David, who carefully writes it in the book.

DAVID   Thanks. And Trev owes nineteen and six.

STEVEN   Nineteen and six? That means he's only paid sixpence. You've only paid sixpence!

TREV   I know. I don't think I'm going to be able to get the money, Maggie. I've tried.

STEVEN   Tried what?

TREV   Tried everything. Tried to get a job. Tried to get a paper   20 round. Couldn't get one. Tried asking my mum.

MICHAEL   You didn't tell her what the money was for?

TREV   No, I didn't tell her.

MICHAEL   What did you say?

TREV	I said, 'gis a quid, mum.'
MICHAEL	What did she say?
TREV	She said … (***Trev*** *whispers in* **Michael's** *ear.*)
MICHAEL	Oh … right.
STEVEN	Well, if he can't pay, he can't go to London, can he?
MAGGIE	He's got to go to London. We've all got to go to London. That's the whole point. We're all going.
STEVEN	'Cept Christine.
MAGGIE	Yeah, 'cept her.
STEVEN	And Trev.
MICHAEL	No. He's got to come. Maggie's right. It's the whole point … in a couple of weeks' time, it'll be the summer holidays and after that … we'll all be … this is the last time … this is the last time …
JEN	… that we'll all be together.
	Long pause. They go still and look at each other.
MICHAEL	Yeah. Look I've still got five bob left from my birthday money. I'll put that in for you, Trev.
JEN	I've got some dinner money. Here.
	Money starts to be handed in to Michael.
STEVEN	Oh, bloody bugger.
	He hands some coins in.
MICHAEL	(*Counting.*) Seventeen and six. We're nearly there. You're nearly there, Trev.
JACKIE	That two bob you had for your bus fare on Eleven Plus day, Trev …
TREV	Yeah?

JACKIE	I've been looking after it for you. Here.
MICHAEL	That's it, nineteen and six. You've made it, Trev. You're going to London!
TREV	Am I?
MICHAEL	Yes.
TREV	(*Shouting.*) I'm going to London!

A kid runs on holding a newspaper.

KID	Maggie ... Maggie ... look.
MAGGIE	What ... what is it?
KID	Read that ...
MAGGIE	'YURI ON HIS WAY ... The Soviet news agency has announced ... details today of Astronaut Yuri Gagarin's ... planned visit ... guest of the Foundry Workers' Union ... arriving Tuesday 12th July ... arriving Tuesday 12th July! That's next week! That's next bloody Tuesday he's coming! Yuri's coming!
MICHAEL	Oh blimey, Maggie! This is it!

60

ACT 2 ❖ SCENE 8

MICHAEL	I can't wait, Maggie. It's going to be … I can't wait. Look, I've got a train timetable and if we catch the 8.30 then everybody can just set off as if they were going to school and instead of going to school they could all just go to the station … and no one will know 'til it's too late. By the time they realise, we'll be on our way … to London. Course there'll be trouble when we get home but who cares, eh?
MAGGIE	Yeah, who cares?
MICHAEL	Andrews'll go mad. I'd just love to see his face. Miss Green'll have to go and fetch him and he'll come into the classroom and there'll be no one there. Completely empty and he'll look at his watch and he'll look at Green … and panos time! They won't know what to do. Rows and rows of empty desks. A whole class disappeared.
MAGGIE	'Cept Christine.
MICHAEL	Yeah, 'cept her.
MAGGIE	She'll tell, won't she?
MICHAEL	Course she will but it won't matter. It'll be too late. We'll be in London.
MAGGIE	Yeah.
MICHAEL	I can't wait. This is going to be … this is all 'cos of you, Maggie.
MAGGIE	What do you mean?
MICHAEL	This is all 'cos of you. None of this would have happened without you. This whole Yuri thing. It's all 'cos of you.
MAGGIE	I'm going to be in really big trouble, aren't I?
MICHAEL	We all are. Who cares?

MAGGIE	No, but they're going to blame me, aren't they?
MICHAEL	What can they do? You're leaving in two weeks.
	Long pause.

30

MAGGIE	Remember the moonlight swimming club?
MICHAEL	Oh, yeah. That was a good club that was.
MAGGIE	Why was it good?
MICHAEL	Well, it was exciting. You made us all hide our swimming things under the bushes on Top Field. We had food and stuff all stored up and we had secret call signs.
MAGGIE	And badges. You made the badges.
MICHAEL	And on the night we all had to go to bed with bits of string tied round our ankles and going out the bedroom window so we could wake each other up by pulling on the string and we were going to meet up on Top Field and eat all the food and then climb over the swimming pool wall and …

40

MAGGIE	… swim in the moonlight.
MICHAEL	Yeah.
MAGGIE	We never did though. We never went swimming. No one came and pulled the string. No one woke up and it rained in the night and all the towels and food went soggy.
MICHAEL	Yeah.
MAGGIE	So how come the moonlight swimming club was a great club if we never went swimming in the moonlight?

50

MICHAEL	It was exciting … planning it … organising it … looking forward to it.
MAGGIE	*(Pause.)* I never thought he'd come.
MICHAEL	What?
MAGGIE	I never thought he'd really come to England.

MICHAEL	Oh.
MAGGIE	I've never been to London. What if we don't know where to go?
MICHAEL	We'll ask a policeman.
MAGGIE	What if we miss him? We don't even know what time he's coming.
MICHAEL	We'll find out.
MAGGIE	What if someone gets lost? What if someone gets run over? What if something goes wrong?
MICHAEL	It won't. Nothing'll go wrong. It's going to be alright. Honestly. You're bound to be a bit nervous. Think about Yuri. Sitting there on top of his rocket waiting to go up into space. Nobody knew what would happen. Nobody knew if the human body could stand all that force and everything. Some people said the human body would just explode … with all the pressure and everything. They weren't even sure if they could bring him back, and he knows all this and he's sitting there on the top of his rocket and when the moment comes he shouts out 'Poyekhali!' and off he goes.
MAGGIE	Bloody Yuri. Wish I'd never heard of him. I'm sick to death of bloody Yuri.
MICHAEL	Maggie, don't. Don't talk like that. Everything's going to be OK.
MAGGIE	It's easy for you to say that. You're not the one that's going to get into trouble. You're not the one they're going to blame. You're not the one who's going to lose her place at the grammar.
MICHAEL	What?
MAGGIE	And don't say they can't because they can. A girl once did something and she lost her place. They wouldn't let her go.
MICHAEL	I thought you weren't bothered about that? I thought you didn't care? You said it didn't matter.

MAGGIE	Of course it matters.
MICHAEL	Maggie, we've got to go to London. Maggie, listen to me. We've got to go. What about Yuri? He's expecting us. We can't let Yuri down.

90

MAGGIE	Oh, don't be so childish. We're not letting him down.
MICHAEL	We are letting him down.
MAGGIE	No, we're not.
MICHAEL	He wrote to us.
MAGGIE	No, he didn't.
MICHAEL	What?
MAGGIE	Nothing.
MICHAEL	What did you say?
MAGGIE	Nothing.
MICHAEL	He never wrote did he? It was you, wasn't it? WASN'T IT?

100

MAGGIE	Yes.
MICHAEL	You forged the letter.
MAGGIE	My dad's got a typewriter.
MICHAEL	And the photo?
MAGGIE	From the *Radio Times*. You could send off for them. I signed it with a biro.
MICHAEL	Why?
MAGGIE	I had to. We needed the letter. To get the club going. I had to.
MICHAEL	To get the club going? That's all you cared about, getting the club going. Being in charge. I hate you, Maggie. You were only thinking about yourself, weren't you? You just used Yuri. You never even cared about him. Did you?

110

MAGGIE	Did you?
MICHAEL	Yes.

ACT 2 ❖ SCENE 9

Steven, Trev and Christopher carry on loads of Yuri clobber, including the scrap book.

STEVEN	It's not fair. It's not fair. How could she do that?
CHRISTOPHER	She was alright about it yesterday. Didn't say anything about this yesterday.
TREV	So, does this mean we're not going?
STEVEN	Yes, it means we're not going. Course it means we're not going.
TREV	Why?
STEVEN	'Cos bloody Maggie doesn't want to any more. 'Cos bloody Maggie's changed her mind.
TREV	But we could still go. Even if she's not going, we could still go.
CHRISTOPHER	How could we?
TREV	We could go by ourselves. Just us. Couldn't we?
STEVEN	We couldn't go without Maggie.
TREV	Why not. What's so special about Maggie? We could do it without her.
CHRISTOPHER	No.
TREV	Why not?
STEVEN	We just couldn't, alright?
TREV	But …
STEVEN	WE JUST COULDN'T … we couldn't do it. OK?
TREV	OK.

STEVEN	I never wanted to go anyway. Smelly old place, London is. I never wanted to go there in the first place. Who wants to go to London?
CHRISTOPHER	Not me.
STEVEN	Yeah. Better off here, we are. And who wanted to see old Yuri anyway? What's so special about him? Bloody old Russian, that's all he is.
CHRISTOPHER	Bloody old communist Russian, that's all he is.
STEVEN	*(Opening the scrap book.)* Yeah, look at him. Bloody old Russian in a helmet. Who wanted to see him anyway? Look at him, laughing away. Bet he never even did it.
CHRISTOPHER	Bet that's why he's laughing. He's laughing his head off 'cos he never did it.
STEVEN	Don't laugh at us, mate. *(He rips out a large picture of Yuri's face from the scrap book.)* We know your game. Sitting there in your helmet, pretending you went up into space when you never even went up there.
CHRISTOPHER	He's lucky we're not going to London 'cos we'd have told him, wouldn't we?
STEVEN	Yeah, well that's the end of you, mate. *(He rips the picture into pieces. He's crying now.)*
CHRISTOPHER	Yeah. We've just about had enough of you. *(Rips out another page.)*
STEVEN	*(Rips out more pages.)* You can stop laughing,'cos its not funny any more. The joke's over.
	Steven and **Christopher** rip the scrap book to pieces. **Trev** looks on, horrified.

30

40

50

ACT 2 ❖ SCENE 10

Maggie *is on Top Field in exactly the same position as at the start of the play.* **Jen** *slowly approaches her.*

JEN	I've been watching you for ages. You've been up here for ages. Want an apple?
MAGGIE	No.
JEN	Michael's gone missing.
MAGGIE	I heard.
JEN	He hasn't been seen since this morning.
MAGGIE	I know.
JEN	His mum's called the police.
MAGGIE	Yeah.
JEN	They're going to do a search party thingy.
MAGGIE	They won't find him.
JEN	Why not?
MAGGIE	'Cos he's not here.
JEN	Isn't he?
MAGGIE	No.
JEN	Where is he then?
MAGGIE	London.
JEN	What?
MAGGIE	He's gone to London … to see Yuri.
JEN	What, by himself?
JEN	Did he tell you?

MAGGIE	No.
JEN	Then how do you know?
MAGGIE	'Cos I do. 'Cos I know him. 'Cos he wouldn't give up.
JEN	So you think he just went, all by himself?
MAGGIE	Yeah.
JEN	To London? All by himself?
MAGGIE	Yeah.
JEN	Blimey.
MAGGIE	Yeah.
JEN	So, once he's seen Yuri, what d'you think he'll do?
MAGGIE	I think he'll come back.
JEN	Tonight?
MAGGIE	Yeah.
JEN	Is that why you're waiting up here?
MAGGIE	Yeah.
JEN	Can I wait with you?
MAGGIE	If you want to. If you're still talking to me.
JEN	I'm not cross.
MAGGIE	Everybody else is.
JEN	Yeah. They're disappointed. They thought they were going …
MAGGIE	… to London. I'm sorry.
JEN	Never mind. We had fun though, doing it. All the Yuri stuff. It was good fun.
MAGGIE	Was it?

30

40

JEN	Yeah. It was the best club I've ever been in. I love being in a club like that, I do. You know, when we're all together, doing things. It's lovely. Do you know what I mean?
MAGGIE	Yeah.
JEN	Is it finished now, Maggie? The Yuri fan club. Is that the end of it?
MAGGIE	Yeah.
JEN	You'll be going to the grammar soon won't you?
MAGGIE	Yeah. Suppose so.
JEN	Yeah. *(Long pause.)* I gotta go.

Jen gets up to leave, then stops.

JEN	He was brave though, wasn't he? Going up there all by himself.
MAGGIE	Yeah.

*Jen slowly exits. It's getting dark. **Maggie** climbs up on the mound and starts to count slowly. When she gets to fifteen, **Michael** appears in the distance. He's got a duffle bag on his back and he's carrying a Thermos flask.*

MAGGIE	Hello. I've been waiting for you. I knew you'd come. I just said to Jen he'll come back tonight and I'm waiting for him. And you did. Yeah. What happened? Did you? Did you see him then? Michael? Did you see Yuri? You didn't see him, did you? Bet you got lost in London, or … or you got on the wrong train and never even got there. Yeah, I bet you never even got there. You're going to be in ever such a lot of trouble, you are. Your dad's going to kill you. They've been looking for you all day. *(Pause.)* Do you want a biscuit? *(Pause.)* Did you see him then? Michael, what happened?
MICHAEL	I broke my Thermos flask. Dropped it. I think it's all smashed up inside. It's my dad's. Do you know if you can mend them?

MAGGIE	What?
MICHAEL	Thermos flasks. Can you mend them? I don't think you can. Think I'll just put it in a bin.

80

MAGGIE	Are you going to tell me or what? *(Pause.)* Right, I'm going home, I am. I'm going home if you're not going to talk to me. See you tomorrow, yeah? See you tomorrow? Michael?

Michael stares at her. She waits for an answer, gives up and slowly leaves. Michael watches her go then walks to the spot where we first saw Maggie at the start of the play.

MICHAEL   When I was eleven, I had a blue jumper with no sleeves and my hair was all cut short up the sides like this. When I was eleven, we always used to play up here on Top Field. It's a car park now for Asda but when I was eleven, Top Field was … a field … and I used to play up here with Maggie. I used to watch out for her from my bedroom window, and if she came and stood up here on the mound, it'd mean she wanted to see me and I'd start running. I don't see her any more. She went to the grammar school and, well, I don't see her any more. I never told her. I never told her that it was exactly like she said it'd be. *(The Soviet Anthem begins to play in the background.)* There were steps and the sun was shining and a big black car came and there were policemen on motorbikes and the car stopped and someone got out and it was him. And we all cheered and he came across and started shaking hands and I was this close to him and … I could see everything … and I touched him. I touched the spaceman, Maggie. You should have been there.

90

100

The music swells. The lights begin to fade. The images of the playing children reappear. Michael turns towards them and watches for a few seconds. Fade to black.

THE END

ACTIVITIES

THINGS TO TALK ABOUT

1   What do you remember about being in the last year of primary school? Work in groups and jot down on a large sheet of card, as quickly as you can, anything that comes into your head. The following prompts might help you:

- What was on television?
- What music did you like?
- What fashions did you go for?
- What games did you play?
- Can you remember any big news stories?
- Were you interested in any sports?
- What sorts of things did you like/dislike doing in school?

2   Looking back at the things we did as children can feel a bit embarrassing but also quite nice. Take a look at all the things you have written on the card. How do they make you feel?

3   What heroes or idols did you have when you were eleven? Have you ever been a member of a fan club? Talk about why children and young people have heroes and idols. Do you think it is a good thing to have them?

4   What makes some people leaders? What personal attributes does Maggie have that make her a leader in Class 4? Are all of Maggie's characteristics 'good' qualities? What makes a 'good' leader?

5   What do you remember about moving from primary to secondary school? Work in pairs. Face your partner and play 'word tennis' by 'batting' words to each other which capture what you remember feeling. For example:

excited	worried
new uniform	new friends
missing old ones	scary new teachers

6 How would you have felt if you had been in Maggie and Michael's shoes and faced with the prospect of going to a different school from your best friend? Talk about this with a partner and jot down some key words and ideas.

- One of you should adopt the role of Maggie, the other Michael. Each of you should sketch out a monologue in which, as an adult, you explain to an audience what you remember about the summer of 1961, the last time you were with your friend.
- Find a way of intercutting your monologues to make them more dramatically effective.

THINGS TO WRITE ABOUT

7 Choose one of these characters: Maggie, Michael, Trev, Christine.

- Write the comments that Miss Green and the head teacher might have written on their final report.
- Now, imagine the same character wrote an entry in their private diary the night before the Eleven Plus results letter was due to arrive.

8 The audience only hears fragments of each of the children's letters to Yuri Gagarin. What would each whole letter say? This is an exercise in tone and style. Remember, the letters are written by eleven-year-olds to a world-class hero who didn't speak English. So, there are many challenges here for the young writers in terms of:

- being polite and respectful
- trying to use 'grown-up' vocabulary and avoiding colloquialisms that Yuri may not understand
- showing admiration without gushing
- trying to get Yuri to send a reply.

9 When Yuri Gagarin returned to Earth after his 108-minute flight in space on 12th April 1961, this is what he said:

> I must say the view of the horizon is quite unique and very beautiful. It is possible to see the remarkably colourful change from the light surface of the Earth to the completely black sky in which one can see the stars. This dividing line is very thin, just like a belt of film surrounding the

Earth's sphere. It is of a delicate blue colour. And this transition from the blue to the dark is very gradual and lovely. It is difficult to put it into words.

When I emerged from the shadow of the Earth, the horizon looked different. There was a bright orange strip along it, which again passed into a blue hue and once again into a dense black colour.

I did not see the Moon. The Sun in outer space is ten times brighter than here on Earth. The stars are visible very well they are bright and distinct. The whole picture of the heavens is much more contrasty than when seen from Earth.

- What clues are there here that this is reported speech rather than something Gagarin wrote?

- Are there clues here that tell you that Gagarin's words have been translated into English from their original Russian?

- What does the style of the language tell you about the kind of report Gagarin is most used to making?

- Imagine that you were the first person to see planet Earth from outer space. Write your description of the experience.

10 A *clerihew* is a four-line poem about a person in which the first and last two lines rhyme. It's named after its inventor, Edmund Clerihew Bentley. Here's a good example:

Neil Armstrong

Wasn't on the moon for long

But in that time he left behind

A giant footstep for mankind.

John Foster

Try and write one about Yuri Gagarin.

Bringing the Play to Life

11 What make us different from everyone else are our idiosyncrasies – that is, the very particular way we do things. Each of the play's young characters needs to come across as an individual in order to make them dramatically interesting – that is, good to watch and listen to on stage. They must have their own way of speaking and moving and might perhaps have a particular gesture or facial expression.

- Working in groups of four or five, select a character each. Find a line from the play that you think only that character would say.

- Practise a way of saying the line that you think would suit the character. Try to find a gesture and/or facial expression that the character would make in conjunction with the line.

- Move around the room in a way that you think would suit the character, say your line to everyone you meet and listen to the line that is said back to you. It's important that you only say the line and do not say which character you are playing.

- After a few minutes, gather together with classmates who you think have chosen the same character as you. Share your lines, gestures and expressions again, and talk about why you chose them.

12 One way of getting into a character is to give them a *back story* – that is, invent extra details of their life that fit with what they appear to be like in the play.

- Divide into five groups. Each group should take responsibility for one of the following characters:

    Jen   Jackie   Val   Christopher   Trev

- Draw a simple outline of a person on a sheet of card. Look through the script again, picking out and re-reading the scene in which your group's character appears. Using one colour pen, write inside the outline everything you think the script tells you about the character.

- Now, using a different colour pen, add details of your own that you think would help an actor play the character.

- Set up five chairs in your working space. One of your group should volunteer to adopt the character. As a class, move around the space, hot-seating the different characters. Find out what they are like as people. Those playing the characters can add new details of their lives in order to answer the questions they are asked.

- Talk about the extent to which the characters became increasingly believable in this exercise.

13 The audience of *The Spaceman* gains only brief insights into the home lives of a few of the characters, for example: Christine being rewarded with a new bicycle (page 15), Jackie's mum reading the post in bed (page 17), Christopher talking to his mum (page 20). But what about Michael, Maggie, and Trevor?

- Working in small groups, create a sequence of three still images depicting an eleven-year-old child and his or her family:
  - waiting for the postman on 'the big day'
  - reading the letter
  - responding to its contents.
- Perform the sequence again. Think of it as a cartoon strip. This time, add either two speech balloons and one thought bubble, or one speech balloon and two thought bubbles, to each frame.

14 What do you think the most dramatic moments in the play are? The moment when Maggie challenges the head teacher about him not allowing the letters to be sent to Russia (page 36)? When Val tells Christine that panos actually means diarrhoea (pages 49–50)?

- In groups, choose a dramatic moment from the play and create a still image of it. Imagine that this image will be used to advertise a production of the play, so ensure that each character is shown in detail (think about their idiosyncrasies).
- Take it in turns to step out of the image to say aloud what your character is thinking at that moment.

15 Maggie, Michael and the rest of Class 4 would be in their sixties now. Perhaps they would have grandchildren of their own. Imagine that someone has organised a reunion for Class 4.

● Take some time to invent a character of your own (not one of the named characters in the play). Did you pass the Eleven Plus? Were you in the Yuri fan club? What have you gone on to do as an adult?

● As a whole class, improvise the small talk at the reunion. Topics might include:

– what you remember of Maggie, Michael, Christine, Trev and the others that haven't shown up

– what you have heard through the grapevine that they are doing now

– what you think about recent news reports that the Eleven Plus might be reintroduced and children sent to different types of school depending on their results.

16 Undertake some research into how eleven-year-olds speak and behave. Rob John, the author of *The Spaceman*, recalls:

When rehearsing the first production, we ran a drama workshop for a Year 6 class from a local primary school. Cast members worked in small groups with ten- and eleven-year-olds and watched the way they moved, spoke, and interacted with each other and with adults. It completely changed the way they perceived children of this age and the spaceman characters started to take shape from that day.

● In 1964 a documentary called *Seven Up* examined the lives of a group of seven-year-old children. The same group has been filmed every seven years since. Searching for *Seven Up* on YouTube will give you an excellent insight into what the world of Maggie, Michael and the others would have been like.

● Look up *Of Time and the City* by Terence Davies and *One Potato, Two Potato* from 1957. These clips will also give you insights into how children looked and behaved around the time *The Spaceman* is set.

STAGING THE PLAY

17   *The Spaceman* is a memory play. Both the first and the last speeches of the play start with the words, 'When I was eleven …'. This suggests that although the characters the audience actually see on stage are depicted as eleven-year-olds, they need to be played by actors who are older. The characters are certainly children, but perhaps there is an element that they are children that have been put together in the memories of their older selves.

- Take a section of the play and look out for any lines of dialogue that suggest that they have come from the memory of an older person rather than being the sorts of things that eleven-year-olds would actually say.

- In pairs, rehearse the scene in which Maggie and Michael squabble over the biscuit (page 5). Select six to eight lines and learn these off by heart. Experiment with different ways of using your voices, altering the volume, pitch, tone, speed of delivery and use of pauses. Try out different ways of moving in the scene, varying the distance between the two characters. Change your facial expressions and the way you make (or avoid) eye contact. Move towards a polished performance of the short section in which everything you do has been carefully selected and agreed upon.

- Link up with two other pairs of classmates. Present your performances to each other and discuss the ways in which you have interpreted and portrayed the characters.

18   The way the relationship between Maggie and Michael changes is a vital aspect of the play, suggesting an important and painful part of the journey from childhood to adolescence and perhaps also the way that adult decisions (such as the setting of the Eleven Plus exam) can have a destructive impact on young people.

In pairs, read through these sequences:

- Act 1, Scene 6 (pages 21–22) in which they find out how they did in the Eleven Plus.

- Act 2, Scene 2 (pages 43–45) in which Maggie tries to convince Michael that nothing will change between them.

- Act 2, Scene 8 (pages 66–69) in which Michael says he is going to London and Maggie reveals she typed the letter from Yuri.
- Act 2, Scene 10 (pages 72–75) in which Michael returns from London.

Sculpt four still images that capture how Maggie and Michael's relationship changes through these four scenes.

19 All of the adult characters in the play are presented by pre-recorded voices. Why do you think Rob John has written the script in this way? What are the dramatic advantages?

The actors playing the children need to help the audience to imagine these invisible characters by using eye contact to locate the adult characters and give us a sense of their comparative size.

- In groups of up to six, rehearse Act 1, Scene 9 (pages 31–32) in which the head teacher speaks to the children who have passed the Eleven Plus. One of you should read the lines for the head teacher but not physically play a part in the scene. Rather, you should also act as a director, advising the children where to focus their attention and how to respond to the unseen presence of the head teacher.

20 The play rapidly moves between settings: a field, a classroom, the head teacher's office, a bus stop and at least four different homes.

How might these locations be shown without using complex and expensive scenery, which will take time to change?

The opening stage direction reads:

The only set is a very long table, which will serve for mound, benches, school desks and any other structure required by the production.

You will have to think about how this will work and if you will, in fact, need to use anything else. Draw up a table like the one below and make notes on how each scene might be simply but effectively suggested.

Scene	Location	Stage furniture / Props / Lighting
	Top Field	

21 The opening stage direction suggests that an image of children playing in 1961 is used to help set the time period of the play. Use the internet to research images from the early 1960s. Pay attention to the fashions of the time. Find out what was happening in the news. What sort of music was popular? You might choose to create a montage of images to project as an introduction to a performance or use in a foyer display to help the audience understand more about the context of *The Spaceman*.

Exploring the Issues

The Eleven Plus

In 1944, at the end of World War Two, there was a major overhaul of the British education system. Schools were divided into primary and secondary schools, and a 'transfer test' was introduced to see which sort of secondary school pupils would be best suited to. This test became known as the Eleven Plus exam.

The idea was to have three types of school:

- Grammar schools, which would teach a highly academic curriculum, focusing on literature, classics and mathematics.
- Technical high schools, which would prepare their pupils to become scientists, engineers and technicians.
- Secondary modern schools, which would train pupils in practical skills.

In most parts of the country, it didn't work out like that. Very few counties introduced technical high schools, and the Eleven Plus became a way of sifting out 'the brightest and best' for the grammar schools, while secondary moderns 'got the rest'! Critics pointed out that the system was unfair on a number of points:

- Grammar schools were given more money than secondary moderns.
- There were more grammar schools in the south of England than anywhere else.
- There were more places for boys in grammar schools than girls.
- Some of the questions on the Eleven Plus exam were pitched towards middle-class children: for example, some questions were about classical composers and the role of different household servants.

By the middle of the 1960s, many counties had replaced the original Eleven Plus exam with a number of different sorts of verbal and non-verbal reasoning tests. In 1976, the official policy was to introduce comprehensive schools. However, there are still over 160 grammar schools in England and the arguments about whether children should be 'selected' to go to different types of secondary school continue.

22 Talk to family members and other adults about the Eleven Plus. Did your parents or grandparents have to take it? What are their views on it?

23 Some counties in England still have the Eleven Plus exam and some people think it should be reintroduced for all children. What do you think?

- As a whole class, take it in turns to say 'yes' if you think such an exam could be a good thing, or 'no' if you are against it. You might choose to play Devil's advocate – that is, when you say you agree or disagree with something even though you don't really!

- Now, take it in turns to give reasons. A reason 'for' must be followed by a reason 'against', and so on. You must take turns!

- After debating in this way for a while, go round again and say either 'yes' or 'no' in response to the question 'Is the Eleven Plus exam a good thing?' It's OK to have changed your mind as a result of listening to the different reasons given in the debate.

24 Read this poem by Roger McGough. It's called 'Streemin'.

Im in the botom streme
Which meens Im not brigth
dont like reeding
Cant hardly write

but all these divishns
arnt reely fair
look at the cemtery
no streemin there

Do you agree that dividing children on the basis of how good at reading and writing they are isn't fair? If you were in charge of education, how would you organise things?

THE SPACE RACE

In August 2012, *Curiosity* became the first manmade vehicle to land successfully on the surface of Mars, a planet that is around 140 million miles away from Earth. That's quite a feat given that the first ever man-powered flight was made only just over 100 years ago!

The timeline below shows how incredibly quickly the technology of flying has developed and some of the reasons why.

1903	The Wright brothers make the first powered flight. They cover 36.6 metres in 12 seconds.
1909	Louis Blériot crosses the English Channel.
1914–1918	World War One. Aeroplanes are used for the first time in warfare. There is rapid development of technology as each side tries to gain advantage in the air. In 1915, London is bombed by German airships called zeppelins.
1919	Englishmen Alcock and Brown make the first airborne transatlantic crossing in an old bomber from World War One.
1927	American Charles Lindberg makes the first solo airborne crossing of the Atlantic.

1930	Sir Frank Whittle invents the jet engine but is unable to get his invention backed by the Government. The Germans, however, secretly develop the first jet aircraft, which takes its first flight in 1939, just one week before the start of World War Two.
1939–1945	World War Two. Aircraft are used extensively to bomb enemy cities. In 1943, German V2 rockets hit London. They fly too fast to be picked up by radar. The chief designer of the German rocket programme, Wernher von Braun, is captured by the Americans at the end of the war and starts to work on their rocket programme.
1946	The world's two superpowers, the USA and the Soviet Union, become increasingly suspicious and fearful of each other's military might. Winston Churchill says 'an "iron curtain" has descended across the continent' of Europe. The Cold War begins. In America, the fear of 'reds under the bed' leads to a witch-hunt of supposed communist sympathisers.
1957	The Soviet Union becomes the first country to put a manmade object into space when they launch *Sputnik 1*. The USA is horrified by the possibility that they might now be attacked from space. The Space Race begins.

1961	Yuri Gagarin becomes the first human in space.
1961	The USA sites missiles in Italy and Turkey capable of destroying the Soviet capital, Moscow, with nuclear warheads.
1962	The Soviet Union builds missile bases in Cuba, just off the coast of the USA. When Soviet ships carrying missiles to Cuba are spotted, US President John F Kennedy demands that they turn back. The world holds its breath, fearing all-out nuclear war is just hours away. A deal is struck and disaster is averted. The US and Soviet presidents start to talk about joining forces on a programme to land on the Moon, but President Kennedy is assassinated before agreement is reached.
1968	The American *Apollo 8* becomes the first spacecraft to orbit the Moon.

1969	20th July. *Apollo 11* lands on the Moon and Neil Armstrong becomes the first human to set foot on the Moon. The total computing power of the spaceship that went to the Moon was less than that of a modern mobile phone. 
1975	Soviet and American spacecraft link up in orbit. The Space Race is over. The two countries start to work together to build an international space station.

25 Work in a group to make a PowerPoint presentation on one of the following:

The Red Scare	The Space Race
Yuri Gagarin	The Cuban Missile Crisis
The First Moon Landing	The International Space Station

26 Re-read the head teacher's speech in which he explains why he will not let the class send their letters to Yuri (page 36).

- Hot seat a member of your class in the role of the head teacher. Try to get him or her to explain further why he or she thinks writing to the spaceman is unacceptable.

- In pairs, imagine either Maggie or Michael and the head teacher bump into each other some years later. Improvise the conversation they might have, starting with the head teacher saying, 'Ah yes. I remember. You were the spaceman fan, weren't you?'

27 Imagine that Michael and Maggie are called to the head teacher's office after Michael bunked off school in order to go and see Yuri Gagarin. Divide into three groups, each group representing one of the three characters.

- In your character group, talk about how you think your chosen character would prepare for this meeting. What points would he or she want to make?

- What would be the best outcome of the meeting for your character?

- What would he or she want to avoid happening at all costs?

- Set up three chairs facing each other. Each group should put forward a volunteer to represent their character in the meeting. These three volunteers should take a seat. The rest of their group should gather behind them.

- Start the meeting by having the head teacher say, 'Good morning, Margaret. Good morning, Michael. I've called you here this morning because …'

- The three players on the chairs should try to keep the meeting going. The rest of their teams must watch and listen carefully but if they think they can help their player by suggesting something to say in the meeting, they may call 'Time out'. The meeting must stop and each team has thirty seconds to advise their player how best to continue.

- The meeting may come to a natural end or, if it starts to feel like things are just going round in circles, stop it.

- Talk about the extent to which each character got what they wanted from the meeting and how they managed (or didn't manage) to achieve their aim.

28   Take a look at these two poems.

The space race! The space race!
What has it all been for?
Stockpiling satellites
To wage a nuclear war?

The space race! The space race!
Wouldn't it have been more worth
Spending all that money
To improve life on Earth?

                    Derek Stuart

The swirling world stands still
As I speed on and on
Through aching space
Of stars and light from yesterday.

I cannot tell you why
I make this search. I only know
The ever-hungry asking
Of the human race.

                    John Kitching

Working as a group, choose one of these poems and find a way of
performing it. This means not just reading the words aloud, but also
adding visual images and movement in order to emphasise its meaning.